Sex, Drugs, and Death

Tammy L. Anderson

Sex, Drugs, and Death: Addressing Youth Problems in American Society explores how youth lifestyles, identities, behaviors, and activities produce a wide range of social problems in contemporary society. The book focuses on the interconnections between three of the most significant youth issues: sexuality, substance use, and suicide. The book pays special attention to the unique pursuits of young people and the locations in which they interact, including virtual places like Facebook and more actual ones such as high school, college, and nightclubs. Patterns among females and males of various class, race, and ethnic backgrounds are also featured prominently in the text, as well as how sociologists think about and study them.

Tammy L. Anderson is a Professor in the Department of Sociology and Criminal Justice at the University of Delaware. She has published many papers on deviance, drugs, music scenes, gender, race, and young people. Her recent book *Rave Culture: The Alteration and Decline of a Philadelphia Music Scene* (2009) showcases her qualitative approach to understanding these topics.

Framing 21st Century Social Issues

The goal of this new, unique Series is to offer readable, teachable "thinking frames" on today's social problems and social issues by leading scholars. These are available for view on http://routledge.custom gateway.com/routledge-social-issues.html.

For instructors teaching a wide range of courses in the social sciences, the Routledge *Social Issues Collection* now offers the best of both worlds: originally written short texts that provide "overviews" to important social issues *as well as* teachable excerpts from larger works previously published by Routledge and other presses.

As an instructor, click to the website to view the library and decide how to build your custom anthology and which thinking frames to assign. Students can choose to receive the assigned materials in print and/or electronic formats at an affordable price.

Body Problems
Running and Living Long in a Fast-Food Society
Ben Agger

Sex, Drugs, and Death
Addressing Youth Problems in American Society
Tammy Anderson

The Stupidity Epidemic
Worrying About Students, Schools, and America's Future
Joel Best

Empire Versus Democracy
The Triumph of Corporate and Military Power
Carl Boggs

Contentious Identities
Ethnic, Religious, and Nationalist Conflicts in Today's World
Daniel Chirot

The Future of Higher Education
Dan Clawson and Max Page

Waste and Consumption
Capitalism, the Environment, and the Life of Things
Simonetta Falasca-Zamponi

Rapid Climate Change
Causes, Consequences, and Solutions
Scott G. McNall

The Problem of Emotions in Societies
Jonathan H. Turner

Outsourcing the Womb
Race, Class, and Gestational Surrogacy in a Global Market
France Winddance Twine

Changing Times for Black Professionals
Adia Harvey Wingfield

Why Nations Go to War
A Sociology of Military Conflict
Mark Worrell

Sex, Drugs, and Death

Addressing Youth Problems in American Society

Tammy L. Anderson

University of Delaware

Routledge
Taylor & Francis Group

NEW YORK AND LONDON

First published 2011
by Routledge
270 Madison Avenue, New York, NY 10016

Simultaneously published in the UK
by Routledge
2 Park Square, Milton Park, Abingdon, Oxon OX14 4RN

Routledge is an imprint of the Taylor & Francis Group, an informa business

Typeset in Garamond and Gill Sans by EvS Communication Networx, Inc.

Library of Congress Cataloging in Publication Data
Anderson, Tammy L., 1963–
Sex, drugs, and death : addressing youth problems in American society /
Tammy L. Anderson.
p. cm. — (Framing 21st century social issues)
1. Youth—United States—Social conditions—21st century. 2. Youth—Sexual
behavior—United States. 3. Substance abuse—United States. 4. Youth—
Suicidal behavior—United States. I. Title.
HQ796.A685 2011
306.70835'0973—dc22
2010029005

ISBN13: 978-0-415-89205-6 (pbk)
ISBN13: 978-0-203-83422-0 (ebk)

Contents

Series Foreword   vii

Preface   ix

I.   Understanding Youth Social Problems   1

II. Youth Problems Associated with Sexuality   11

III. Substance Abuse   20

IV. Suicide   35

V.   Sociological Solutions to Youth Problems   44

     References   53

     Glossary/Index   63

Series Foreword

The world in the early 21st century is beset with problems—a troubled economy, global warming, oil spills, religious and national conflict, poverty, HIV, health problems associated with sedentary lifestyles. Virtually no nation is exempt, and everyone, even in affluent countries, feels the impact of these global issues.

Since its inception in the 19th century, sociology has been the academic discipline dedicated to analyzing social problems. It is still so today. Sociologists offer not only diagnoses; they glimpse solutions, which they then offer to policy makers and citizens who work for a better world. Sociology played a major role in the civil rights movement during the 1960s in helping us to understand racial inequalities and prejudice, and it can play a major role today as we grapple with old and new issues.

This series builds on the giants of sociology, such as Weber, Durkheim, Marx, Parsons, Mills. It uses their frames, and newer ones, to focus on particular issues of contemporary concern. These books are about the nuts and bolts of social problems, but they are equally about the frames through which we analyze these problems. It is clear by now that there is no single correct way to view the world, but only paradigms, models, which function as lenses through which we peer. For example, in analyzing oil spills and environmental pollution, we can use a frame that views such outcomes as unfortunate results of a reasonable effort to harvest fossil fuels. "Drill, baby, drill" sometimes involves certain costs as pipelines rupture and oil spews forth. Or we could analyze these environmental crises as inevitable outcomes of our effort to dominate nature in the interest of profit. The first frame would solve oil spills with better environmental protection measures and clean-ups, while the second frame would attempt to prevent them altogether, perhaps shifting away from the use of petroleum and natural gas and toward alternative energies that are "green."

These books introduce various frames such as these for viewing social problems. They also highlight debates between social scientists who frame problems differently. The books suggest solutions, both on the macro and micro levels. That is, they suggest what new policies might entail, and they also identify ways in which people, from the ground level, can work toward a better world, changing themselves and their lives and families and providing models of change for others.

Readers do not need an extensive background in academic sociology to benefit from these books. Each book is student-friendly in that we provide glossaries of terms for the uninitiated that are keyed to bolded terms in the text. Each chapter ends with questions for further thought and discussion. The level of each book is accessible to undergraduate students, even as these books offer sophisticated and innovative analyses.

Tammy Anderson addresses issues that concern every parent and teenager—youth culture! Focusing on substance abuse, sexuality and suicide, Anderson explores the intriguing world of our kids with an anthropologist's eye for detail. Many critics agree that children grow up too fast, with too many adult expectations, neglecting the fact that childhood and adolescence are fragile developmental stages. It is difficult to expect kids to deal with their emerging sexuality and with omnipresent drugs without sometimes going off the rails. Anderson concludes with constructive suggestions, at both the policy and individual levels, for easing the burden of adolescents. She empathizes and doesn't judge.

Preface

Sex, Drugs, and Death: Addressing Youth Problems in Contemporary Society discusses three broad areas of youth behaviors that are deemed problematic, yet, at times, are celebrated in U.S. culture: sex and sexuality, substance use, and suicide. The book takes a cursory look into these problem areas for three main reasons. First, sexuality, substance abuse, and suicide present an opportunity to teach readers about the unique ways sociologists study youth and the problems they face. This includes helping the reader understand how youth behavior gets defined as problematic in the first place as well as learning the theories and methods sociologists use to study and address them. Unlike other disciplines, sociology allows us to comprehend how individuals and groups are connected to the communities, societies, nations, and cultures within which they live. Understanding this relationship is critically important for solving social problems in both the short and the long term. Second, these three issues help elucidate how youth and other social problems are patterned (usually by social group) in our society and how sociologists can help identify what those patterns are so that effective remedies can be put forth. Third, and perhaps most importantly, sexuality, substance abuse, and suicide are linked in distinctive ways and highlighting this point will help readers see that such connections are common to social problems in general. Chapter I describes the sociological approach to youth social problems and briefly explains how and why sociologists look for patterns among groups and connections between problems regarding sex, drug use, and suicide. Chapters II to IV focus specifically on sexuality, drug use, and suicide in turn, while staying focused on the book's objectives. Chapter V discusses solutions to youth social problems.

1:   Understanding Youth Social Problems

✤

Introduction

U.S. society in the 21st century is decidedly youth-oriented. The well-being of youth is one of the most central values of our society and culture. While birthing and raising children fundamentally shapes our existence, youth also signifies a lifestyle and aesthetic to which adults aspire. Increasingly, we wish to look, think, and act like young people as much as possible. Industries of all kinds sell older Americans products and services promising a return to youth or younger state. Symbolically then, youth is relevant to all of us since we live in a culture that prioritizes young people and strive to be like them, i.e., youthful.

While youth is both a group of people that demands top priority in society and a sort of 'state' or period with a highly valued aesthetic, lifestyle, and attitude, youth—in both of these forms—is also demonized and heavily monitored and controlled. The monitoring and controlling of youth makes some sense, given the societal importance placed on them/it. However, the viewpoint of youth, youth activities and styles as dangerous and problematic is more curious since they are simultaneously celebrated in our daily lives.

In this book, I look at three broad areas of youth behaviors that are deemed problematic, yet, at times, are celebrated as well: sex and sexuality, substance use, and suicide. Why focus on these three youth problems when there are many others (e.g., illiteracy, delinquency, and child poverty) needing attention? Three reasons justify my effort and serve as objectives of this book. First, sexuality, substance abuse, and suicide present an opportunity to teach readers about the unique ways sociologists study youth and the problems they face. This includes helping the reader understand how youth behavior gets defined as problematic in the first place, as well as learning the theories and methods sociologists use to study and address them. Unlike other disciplines, sociology allows us to comprehend how individuals and groups are connected to the communities, societies, nations, and cultures within which they live. Understanding this relationship is critically important for solving social problems. Second, these three issues help elucidate how youth and other social problems are patterned (usually by social group) in our society and how sociologists can help identify what those patterns are so that effective remedies can be put forth. Third, and perhaps most importantly, sexuality, substance abuse, and suicide are linked in distinctive ways and highlighting this point will help readers see that such connections are common to social problems in general. My focus on the connections between these three youth problems, however, means that there will inevitably be topics related to sex, drugs, and suicide that I can't discuss. Thus, the book should be read as a sociological treatment of three youth problems that are exceptionally patterned and interconnected.

Chapter I describes the sociological approach to youth social problems and briefly explains how and why sociologists look for patterns among groups and connections between problems regarding sex, drug use, and suicide. Chapters II to IV focus specifically on sexuality, drug use, and suicide in turn, while staying focused on the book's objectives. Chapter V discusses solutions to youth social problems.

How Sociologists View and Study Youth Social Problems

Many sociologists view youth problems as being **socially constructed** rather than absolute or objective facts. This means that matters such as teen pregnancy and underage drinking are defined socially, not by nature, as problematic behaviors by certain people for a variety of reasons. People, usually influential or powerful ones, then use various techniques to convince the rest of us to see things their way and to accept their definitions of "youth problems." For example, it was not always against the law for 18-year-olds to consume alcoholic beverages. Between 1970 and 1975, 29 states lowered the minimum drinking age to 18, 19, or 20 (Wechsler and Sands, 1980). Scientists began studying the effects of the lowered drinking age in these places and found increased injury and death to teens from alcohol-related car accidents (Cucchiaro, Ferreira, and Sicherman 1974; Douglass, Filkins, and Clark 1974; Wagenaar, 1983, 1993; Whitehead, 1977; Whitehead et al. 1975; Williams et al. 1974). A **moral crusade** by parents' groups to change minimum drinking age laws followed under the guise of "protecting" the next generation. President Reagan used the 1984 Uniform Drinking Age Act to force the states to change their drinking age laws back to 21 in order to receive federal highway monies. All did by 1988.

Today, youth drinking is believed to cause many problems, not simply teen death and injury. Yet, youth drinking is condoned and even promoted by other institutions and alcohol stakeholders in our society. Consider advertising. The Center for Alcohol Marketing and Youth (2008) discovered that between 2001 and 2007, alcohol marketing on youth-oriented television programs had increased a whopping 38 percent. Their annual study found that "In 2007, approximately one out of every five alcohol advertisements was placed on programming that youth ages 12 to 20 were more likely per capita to see than adults of the legal drinking age." The shifts in minimum drinking laws and conflicting messages from private sector industry about youth drinking are, therefore, good examples to understand what sociologists call the social construction of social problems.

Sociologists use theories about how things in society or our culture (let us call them "environmental" factors) influence individuals and groups to explain youth social problems. Unlike natural scientists or even psychologists, sociologists do not explain or study sexuality, drug use, and suicide by looking exclusively at individuals and their characteristics. Instead, they most often focus on **environmental factors** that can influence our lives in ways we don't often recognize. Sociologists' explanations come in the form of **theories**. Whether grand or modest, theories feature **concepts** with relationships to each other. Concepts are abstract, mental images of phenomena that can usually be indicated by something more measurable in the real world. Peer pressure is one such concept and sociologists have theorized that it helps explain a variety of youth problems, including premarital sex, teen pregnancy, and substance use.

Let's go back to underage drinking to illustrate the sociological way of thinking. Student culture on most college campuses shapes motivations to drink and provides many opportunities for underage people to get drunk. So, if you want to know why young people violate drinking laws and engage in dangerous illegal behavior, sociologists might recommend looking not at the 18-year-olds' biological makeup or self-esteem, but rather to the cultural norms and values he or she is exposed to by certain social groups (e.g., fraternities and sororities) or in certain situations or settings (campus parties or local bars). In short, sociologists understand youth social problems as having cultural, social, and economic origins or ties. The causes that sociologists theorize to have an impact on things like underage drinking or suicide are often external to the individual, i.e., they are not biological, genetic or psychological traits possessed by them. Instead, these explanations direct our attention away from people to both the immediate and more distant social worlds in which they live.

While sociological theories often focus on environmental explanations, others look at individuals to clarify social problems. Such **micro-level** theories explain youth problems using the characteristics or experiences of people or those close to them, e.g., parents and peers. Such explanations are attractive, for many reasons, to both researchers and policy makers. For example, by focusing on individuals, micro-level theories lend themselves better to traditional scientific methods, e.g., quantitative studies using surveys and questionnaires administered to drug users (see the NSDUH profiled in Chapter III). They enable young people under study to be targeted directly by programs and social policy.

Another important quality of **individual or micro-level explanations** is that they often, but not always, identify causes (i.e., **independent variables**) immediately preceding problem behaviors, instead of focusing on more distant precursors of them. For example, poor decision-making skills occur in close proximity to drug-taking, e.g., youth make "poor" decisions when they use drugs. Factors like this are perceived as more "direct" causes, making them attractive to policy makers when fashioning interventions.

Major Sociological Theories

Sociology has three main theories to explain youth and other social problems: **structural functionalism**, **social conflict**, and **symbolic interaction** (Allan 2007; Kimmel and Mahler 2007). Within each of these categories are numerous 'mini-theories' that enrich the broader approach. Structural functionalism and **conflict theories** have focused mostly on the macro picture or things in the social, cultural, and physical environment to explain youth problems, while symbolic interactionism has focused more on social processes and individual interaction to explain the same. All three schools of thought illustrate how sociologists understand youth problems.

Structural Functionalism

To begin, the structural functional paradigm—credited largely to Emile Durkheim, Talcott Parsons, and Robert Merton—views society as a complex system whose parts work together to promote **solidarity** and stability among its population. Humans, especially young people, are believed to be able to thrive under these conditions. Chaos, instability, and **alienation** disrupt society's functioning and are considered undesirable (Durkheim 1933; Merton 1968; Parsons 1951, 1971). Agreement about morality and conformity to norms is required for society's smooth functioning (Durkheim 1947). Conflict about and deviation from norms and values challenge those things. Thus, while some conflict and deviation can be expected among people in a society, too much conflict and deviation will hinder solidarity and stability and thus throw society—and its people—into a state of chaos and alienation (Merton 1968; Parsons 1951, 1971).

Suicide—the subject of Chapter IV in this book—was one of the first social problems to be analyzed from a structural functionalist viewpoint. Writing about societal change after the industrial revolution and the growth of capitalism, Durkheim (1933) warned about the rise of a condition called "**anomie**": the absence of social ties that bind people to society. For him, capitalism's ideology of individualism and preference for organic solidarity (specialized, fragmented social relations highlighting individual difference) weakened social ties among individuals, destabilized society and could lead to chaos.

While Durkheim discussed suicide and other social problems, he did not address youth directly. One of the unique traits of the sociological approach, and a central goal of this book, is the identification of behavioral patterns among groups, e.g., by race, age, gender, social class, and region of the country. Robert Merton (1968), another structural functionalist, targeted youth directly and extended Durkheim's ideas to other social problems with much youth involvement, e.g., crime and drug abuse. Merton was especially interested in explaining delinquency among poor and mixed race/ ethnic youth. He discussed unequal opportunity, something that could produce alienation and, consequently, deviance for many. At issue was young people's access to opportunities for a full, productive life. Merton (1968) argued that such opportunities (economic and educational) were not equally available to all. Instead, access to them was largely a function of one's occupation, neighborhood, age, sex, race, education, and religion. Anomie, alienation or 'strain' emerged when there was a discrepancy between socially approved goals and access to their legitimate attainment. Groups and people with lower status sets suffered less access and, consequently, more strain. Social problems, including those affecting youth, were likely to escalate with increased anomie and unequal opportunity in society.

As indicated above, sociologists also focus on individual actions to explain social problems, including efforts that tie the types of structural explanations of Merton and Durkheim to more psychological issues germane to youth. Robert Agnew's (2006) general strain theory, for example, claims that important 'affect' or psychological variables influence the strain/deviance relationship. Agnew (2006) posited that strain was likely to result when youth place a high value on money, do not view adherence to legitimate norms as a source of status or prestige, and feel they won't be able to achieve financial success through legal channels. This predicament creates anger for some and can lead to problematic behavior. For example, the innovative response of selling drugs to attain goods or the retreatist response of using drugs to escape negative feelings (Anderson 1998a) depends on the individual's emotional response to strain.

Symbolic Interactionism

This brings us to a set of sociological theories focused more on how things happen or on the processes involved in sexual behaviors, drug use, and suicide. The **symbolic interactionist** perspective adopts a micro-level orientation to youth problems, focusing on human interaction in social situations. It sees society as a product of peoples' everyday interactions. In short, people act toward things based on the meaning those things have for them (Blumer 1969). Thus, society and reality are what people make of them.

The social construction of reality is important in understanding youth social problems. For example, interactionists maintain that deviance (i.e., teen sex, drug use, and suicide are types of deviance) is what is so labeled, or what people say it is (Becker 1963). Thus, nothing is inherently deviant or wrong. Such designations are defined by people, who reach those conclusions via shared and contested views of the world, society, and their own experience. This point was made above when reviewing the changing legal definitions of minimum drinking ages.

Symbolic interaction (e.g., **labeling theory**) and **social process theories** (e.g., **social control theory**) are concerned with how people interact and how deviance and drug use unfold over time. For example, these theories focus on how people or groups become involved in sexual behaviors or with drugs and alcohol, how their involvement changes over time, and what might initiate that change. Both social process theories discussed in this section, i.e., labeling theory and social control theory, adopt the structural functionalist tenets about consensus and solidarity.

According to labeling theory, youth drug and alcohol experimentation and use are, for example, not necessarily troublesome initially. Such behaviors become problematic when society officially brands youth as "delinquent" or "deviant" and punishes them harshly. This process of labeling threatens to enmesh young people in drug-abusing careers or lifestyles (Becker 1963; Denzin 1987; Lindesmith 1965, 1968). In other words, when youth are labeled and assumed to possess the negative traits, their involvement in deviance expands because they accept society's pejorative view of them. They called this the **self-fulfilling prophecy** (Cooley 1922, 1998; Lemert 2000). The internalization of negative labels leads to adopting deviant roles (i.e., tasks, behaviors) and identities (Lofland 1969). Interactionists maintain that negative social reactions (label or **stigma**) to individual drug use facilitated more, not less, drug use because individuals would likely internalize the negative labels applied to them and persist in deviant activities. Therefore, labeling theorists were more concerned about the social reaction (i.e., people, officials, agencies, etc.) to drug use, delinquency, and other forms of deviance than about what actually caused or influenced those behaviors in the first place.

When individuals adopt **deviant identities** or roles, they become greatly enmeshed in **deviant careers** (Becker 1963; Lofland 1969). Thus, the so-called middle period of the deviant career features heavy deviant behavior (Reinarman et al. 1997; Stephens 1991). This has deeply concerned both scholars and policy makers, who are interested in understanding and circumventing the experiences, activities, and consequences of active involvement in the illicit drug world, heavy alcohol consumption, promiscuous sex, or self-harm.

A second popular social process theory is social control theory (Gottfredson and Hirschi 1990). Its focus has been almost exclusively on deviant behaviors, such as delinquent acts (theft, vandalism, etc.) and drug use, rather than deviant roles and identities. Unlike labeling theory, social control theory explains original or primary deviance. It does so by asking a rather novel question: Why do people conform? This runs counter to the more common question—why do people deviate or break the law—asked by scholars and policy makers alike.

Intrigued by society's and sociology's innocuous expectation of conformity, Hirschi (1969) began theorizing about deviance by assuming people would violate norms and break the law unless they were actively prevented from doing so. The key to such prevention was effective socialization, which was a long process starting in childhood and lasting into adulthood. Thus, social control theory is considered one about process.

Who and what was responsible for this socialization? Hirschi (1969) and Gottfredson and Hirschi (1990) claimed families, peers, and schools had the most profound impact on each of our lives, especially as children and adolescents. They argued that close associations with parents and siblings, law-abiding peers, and teachers or other school officials, for example, were required to control individuals' behavior. The establishment of a strong moral bond between the juvenile and society, consisting of an attachment to others, commitment to conventional behavior, involvement in conventional activities, and a belief in the moral order and law, promoted conformity and prevented delinquency and other youth problems.

For Hirschi (1969), delinquent behaviors, like drug use, would be a likely outcome of ineffective ties to these things, i.e., improper socialization. Specifically, it is likely to occur if there is inadequate attachment (to parents and school), inadequate commitment (to educational and occupational success), inadequate involvement in conventional activities (e.g., scouting and sports leagues), and inadequate beliefs in such things as the legitimacy and morality of the law.

Social Conflict Theory

Unlike the two prior paradigms that embrace the idea of consensus, **social conflict theories** view society as an arena of inequality and conflict (Allan 2007; Kimmel and Mahler 2007). As indicated above, some interactionist work assumes the same. Conflict arises over disparities in things such as money, property, values, power, and ideology. In a diverse society like the U.S., there are many groups with different cultural values and customs. These cultural traits shape lifestyles, behaviors, identities, and life choices. All of this works to produce cultural conflict in society. Such cultural conflict is related to and exists in addition to more material forms of conflict such as money, wealth, and goods and services.

Conflict theorists are macro-oriented like structural functionalists, albeit they are nearly opposite on how that structure originates and functions. For conflict theorists, society's structure is controlled by those with the greatest economic, social, and cultural assets (Marx 1995; Marx and Engels 1992). Capitalism is an economic system characterized by private ownership of the means of production, from which personal profits can be derived through market competition. This capital enables individuals who own such means of production to rise to positions of power in the public and private sectors, where they continue to create structures that perpetuate their power and interests.

For conflict theorists, social problems, including those studied in this book, are theorized as a response to the alienating conditions of inequality and group (e.g., ethnic and racial minorities) marginalization (Ferrell and Websdale 1999; Quinney 1975). Two modern-day examples of conflict theory's utility in the drug use debate is official lobbying by harm reduction supporters to decriminalize marijuana in favor of individuals' rights to consume it and gang members who claim to sell drugs to empower themselves, their families and their communities (Bourgois 1996; Brotherton 2004).

Social reproduction theory, based on the ideas of the conflict approach, proposes that people acquire at birth and accumulate throughout their lives unequal shares of several types of capital (social, financial, human, and personal) that affect their life chances. Financial capital, i.e., tangible forms of wealth such as money, credit, investment, and assets—the kind Marx (1995; Marx and Engels 1992) discussed—are what most people think of when assessing inequality. Young people are dependent on their parents' financial capital for many things, ranging from basic sustenance needs to school tuition. Parents with greater financial assets can simply pay for better opportunities for their children. Poorer parents cannot provide these things. Thus their children are dependent on social supports (e.g., college tuition, loan programs) from the state. Absent such financial capital and the opportunities it provides, lower-class children may resort to alternative, illegal means to achieve the same things. This was a major premise of Merton's (1968) structural strain theory.

However, social reproduction theorists pointed to other types of capital that widened the inequality/goal attainment gap not previously discussed by Merton and others. One type was human capital, i.e., degrees, education, skills, training, and experience, which is required so that individuals can provide for themselves and others and alter their class position. This Bourdieu (1977) called attention to when criticizing the schools for reproducing class position via channeling youth to certain human capital training programs based on the class positions of their parents.

However, even when lower-class youth managed to attain advanced education and training, they lacked another critical form of capital possessed by the middle and upper classes: social capital, which are one's ties or connections to others who can do things for you or provide special treatment and access (Bourdieu 1977; Bourdieu and Passeron 1990). For example, many college students are unaware of the importance of this premise in understanding inequality and crime in society. Yet, they are aware that jobs or internships they secure often result from the connections their parents, relatives, teachers, and friends have to important others who make recommendations and hiring decisions on their behalf. Research shows that social capital (e.g., networking and access to powerful others) is critically important in securing valuable resources, including college admission and employment. It also shows such capital is not evenly distributed by class, race, ethnicity or gender.

Sociological Methods

Sociologists use a diverse set of research methods to investigate youth social problems empirically. In general, these methods can be classified into two broad categories: quantitative and qualitative. Surveys and experiments are called **quantitative methods** because they are designed to yield numerical measurements of important concepts. Participant observation and in-depth interviewing are called **qualitative methods** because they generally produce textual or non-numerical data. Both quantitative and qualitative methodologies stress that true knowledge is gained by gathering systematic evidence to elucidate a **theory**'s conceptual relationships. Each of the theories described above has concepts it attempts to explain and ideas about their causes. Scientists call outcomes that are to be explained **dependent variables**. Drug use and abuse, sexual behaviors (e.g., teen sex or pregnancy), and suicide are among the more common dependent variables that theories about youth attempt to elucidate. Independent variables are those believed, hypothesized, or discovered to play a role in producing such outcomes. At the theory stage, both independent and dependent variables come in the form of concepts (see page 3).

Understanding sociological theories begins with the discipline's unique focus on these matters. Sociologists have asked somewhat different questions about youth social problems. For example, they've investigated how drug and alcohol use and abuse vary culturally (e.g., by race and ethnicity or between societies), over time (historically), and by geographic location (e.g., the city versus the suburbs). Their objective has not been solely to explain individual behaviors. Sociological theories—like structural functionalism, symbolic interactionism, and conflict theory—utilize broader and often more abstract phenomena and concepts to explain social problems. Causality is more difficult to establish as researchers attempt to measure more abstract concepts and to specify their direct and indirect ties to youth behaviors. Inequality (usually economic) is one such concept. In some form, it is a component of several theories of drug abuse, suicide, and certain sexual behaviors, e.g., teen pregnancy. Yet, how inequality is measured and leads to youth problems is debated among sociologists. Sociological explanations are also challenging for policy makers to utilize and their proposed solutions are difficult to implement. This is because the solutions sociologists advocate require government and private sector resources and change, which is often unpopular with all parties involved.

Conclusions

In this chapter, I introduced the sociological approach to social problems. This approach recognizes that social problems are both subjectively defined and objectively observed. It is important to understand the differences between social constructions of social problems as well as the concrete consequences of them that impact our lives, society, and world. Ascertaining this distinction is made possible by using macro- and micro-level theories to understand how and why things become problematic in society, what patterns and connections exist, and how sociologists can use their tools and perspectives to derive solutions and interventions. These ideas will be considered in the next three chapters on youth sexuality, substance use, and suicide.

There is one last point to consider before we move on to the next chapter. It has to do with the patterning among people and groups. As indicated above, a central purpose of this book, and a unique characteristic of the sociological approach, is discovering that things like teen sex, underage drinking, and self-harm ideation are not randomly distributed among people in our society. Instead, they are patterned by important sociological phenomena, concepts, or variables. Sociologists have shown that demographic background traits (i.e., race, ethnicity, gender, social class, and age) not only help explain different levels of youth involvement in teen pregnancy, non-medical use of prescription drugs, and attempted suicide between whites and blacks, poor and rich, and males and females, but also why and how each group is implicated.

Sociologists' attention to **cultural diversity**—how people's values, lifestyles, and experiences differ by their race, ethnicity, social class, and gender—is a critically important way to understand the patterning of youth social problems. Comprehending such diversity comes by learning how our demographic traits constitute unique identities that connect us to other people and their cultural and social customs.

Intersectionality is a new way of understanding how multi-identities, based in one's race, class, gender, and sexual orientation, impact our lives (Collins 2007; Dill and Zambrana 2009). Intersectionality proposes that all experience is fundamentally structured and shaped by the multiple identities people embrace at any particular moment (Collins 2007; Dill and Zambrana 2009). This counts for youth social problems as well. For example, teen pregnancy may be a different experience for poor minorities than poor whites. **Non-medical abuse of prescription drugs** may impact middle-class whites in ways it does not any other group. The same could be true for coming out as homosexual or getting involved with illegal drugs. Early in my career, for example, I found that the personal identity change processes involved in getting into and out of illegal drugs was informed by the multiple identities of race and gender (Anderson 1998a–d). The point of intersectionality is that youth social problems are shaped by intersectional identities of things like gender, race, social class, age, and sexual orientation. Understanding this is a distinctive quality of sociology and a central objective of this book.

DISCUSSION QUESTIONS

1. How could you use symbolic interaction theory and qualitative methods to study how teens get involved in drug dealing and gangs?
2. What are the benefits of seeing youth social problems as both socially constructed and observable facts?

II: Youth Problems Associated with Sexuality

Introduction

Superbad is a feature film about two high school teenage males who scheme to lose their virginity during a graduation party. The boys set out to find alcohol because they believe it will help them achieve their party goals. The *Superbad* movie grossed more than $120 million in theatres domestically only ten weeks after its release. It was hailed a huge success, leading to numerous other films for its directors and teen actors.

Superbad is not a unique film in any respect. It follows a long line of movies about teenage sexuality (e.g., *American Grafitti*, *American Pie*, *Wild Things*, and *Confession of a Teenage Drama Queen*). The *Superbad* genre tells the teen sexuality tale from the heterosexual boy's standpoint: getting laid and losing one's virginity is the single most important accomplishment of the teen years and earmarks one's transition from boyhood to manhood (and perhaps his masculinity). Films such as *Mean Girls* and *Clueless*, also enormously successful by Hollywood's standards, paint a picture of what many believe is the girls' experience: cattiness between each other over popularity and the pursuit of boys' attention and affection, leading the 'bad' girls to do things they would later regret. A quote by Seth, played by Michael Cera, illustrates the double standard for boys and girls about sexuality and reminds us about the quagmire we face over the glamorization of youth sexuality and its complications. Seth proclaims, "You know when you hear girls say 'Ah man, I was so shit-faced last night, I shouldn't have fucked that guy?' We could be that mistake!"

In general, teens are treated neither as children nor as adults because adolescence is viewed as a transitional period between the two. This transitional period is fraught with many identity problems, not the least of which is defining who one is as a sexual being. According to sociologist Sinikka Elliott (2010: 191), "teen sexual activity is portrayed as fraught with danger, yet sexuality is a pervasive aspect of the American cultural landscape and considered key to identity and fulfillment." For sure, teens face difficult decisions about how they are going to identify and interact with people of the same and opposite sex.

For decades, sociologists have studied the many factors that shape such decisions, locating them in childhood experiences, family structure, high school, and college situations, and in diverse leisure activities. In this chapter, I review some of the factors that shape certain adolescent sexuality issues deemed to be social problems. This review illustrates the unique ways sociologists try to understand adolescence and young adulthood: that something as seemingly personal as sexuality is patterned in knowable ways and that the youth problems of sexuality, substance use, and suicide are fundamentally connected. My discussion begins with problems in childhood and ends with those common in early adulthood. The **sexual victimization** of children serves as our starting point since research shows it has short-term and long-term effects on the child victim's future sexual development, drug and alcohol use and abuse, and self-harm or suicide.

Sexual Victimization of Children

It seems we are bombarded daily with news reports about child sexual abuse tragedies taking place across America. So significant is child sexual abuse to our society and so hated and feared are the sexual offenders who perpetrate it that new sexual offender laws (e.g., **Megan's Law**) dominate legislative agendas and command national attention and significant resources. Official data support this concern. According to the Administration on Children and Families (2008), about 758,289 children were confirmed victims of maltreatment in 2007. The overwhelming majority of these cases involved neglect; however, the report indicates that 9.1 percent, or about 69,000 children, were sexually abused by about 60,253 different offenders.

Today, there are many preconceptions about who these 60,000+ child sexual offenders are. Some include neighbors, coaches, teachers, and priests. However, the most feared and hated sexual predator is the adult stranger who preys on kids at school, playgrounds, and over the Internet. Is this an accurate profile of today's child sexual offender or a misconception resulting from a **moral panic**? The answer is important since knowledge about child sexual abusers is necessary so future abuse can be prevented and the well-being of children and youth ensured.

The majority of child sexual abuse offenders are not random strangers lurking at schools or on the Internet. They are also not commonly our kids' coaches, teachers, or priests. Instead, the majority of child sexual offenders are the children's own parents or those responsible for their care. According to the Administration on Children and Families (2008), nearly 30 percent of child sexual abusers were parents, while another 29 percent were relatives of the child victims. About 4 percent were friends or neighbors and fewer than 1 percent were teachers. The report indicates that about 22 percent of the child abuser perpetrators fell into an "other" category, which could represent strangers. However, even if all of this "other" category was classified so, parents and relatives account for the overwhelming majority of child sexual abusers, thus debunking the popular perceptions about who the perpetrators of child sexual abuse really are.

A recent case in Arizona highlights this point. According to the Associated Press (June 17, 2010), an Arizona couple allegedly physically and sexually assaulted their one-month-old boy, resulting in his death. Nineteen-year-old Staci Lynn Barbosa and 23-year-old Jonathan Edward Vandergriff, the boy's mother and father, were booked into the Mohave County Jail, charged with child molestation, aggravated assault, and sexual conduct with a minor. Barbosa and Vandergriff resemble the more common perpetrators of child sexual abuse in our nation.

That sexual victimization can happen so early in life and within the family makes it extremely problematic since research shows children suffer numerous consequences over the lifecourse from early victimization. For example, children who were maltreated tend to have intercourse and other sexual relations earlier than their non-victimized peers. Black et al. (2009) found that 79 percent and 81 percent of 14- and 16-year-olds who had been maltreated as children were sexually active. Their non-victimized, same aged peers were less likely to be so: 21 percent (14) and 51 percent (16) respectively. Maltreated youth also experience significantly more emotional distress than non-maltreated youth (Black et al. 2009), which other studies tie to substance abuse and suicide. The connections between these problems are discussed more in Chapters III and IV.

Sexual Exploration in High School and Teen Parenting

While sexual activity among teens might be celebrated in popular culture, government officials and other youth advocates view it as troublesome. For example, a variety of government agencies note that youth sexual activity is prevalent in our society today and not something only abused children participate in. According to the Centers for Disease Control (CDC 2010), approximately 46 percent of high school students had sexual intercourse in 2009. Some high school students—14 percent—are quite sexually active, reporting intercourse with four or more partners.

While films like *Superbad* make light of teen sex and even celebrate it, teen sexual activity has long been a concern in our society. This is because it is tied to numerous problems that young people are considered ill-equipped to handle (Maynard 1997). Teen sex results in pregnancy and adolescent parents are often financially, socially, and psychologically not prepared to raise children. Approximately 750,000 adolescents between the ages of 15 and 19 years become pregnant annually. More than 80 percent of these pregnancies are largely unplanned (see Finer and Henshaw 2006). Other problems accompany teen pregnancy. Research shows teen parents suffer reduced educational attainment, fewer employment opportunities, increased likelihood of welfare receipt, and poorer health and developmental outcomes among their infants (Guttmacher 1994).

Teen sex is often careless and risky, performed without contraception, which not only leads to pregnancy, but also to **sexually transmitted diseases** and **HIV**. According to the CDC (2010), there are about 19 million new cases of sexually transmitted diseases in the U.S. each year. More than half of them are among persons between the ages of 15 and 24. Additionally, about 14 percent of this group contracts the HIV virus annually (CDC 2010).

Teenage pregnancy rates vary by race and ethnicity. In general, they are higher among black and Hispanic teenagers than among white teenagers (Ventura et al. 2006). More recent data from the CDC confirms the same race/ethnicity patterns in teen births. Rates of risky sexual behavior are also higher among blacks and Hispanics than among whites (CDC 2000; MacKay, Fingerhut, and Duran 2000). For instance, the **Youth Risk Behavior Survey** (YRBS 2004) shows that the Hispanic teens have sex earlier in life, have more partners and use condoms less than their white counterparts.

Explaining Youth Sexual Activity

Researchers have attempted to explain heterosexual youth's sexual activities in a variety of ways. Studies using large youth surveys like the YRBS tend to focus on individual-level risk factors, such as attitudes, involvement in certain activities, and race, age, and gender (Abma et al. 2004; Finer and Henshaw 2006). In a review of explanations for teen sexual activity, Little and Rankin (2001) identified a wide range of individual and environmental factors that increased the likelihood that youth would engage in premarital sex. For example, teen sex was more likely to occur among teens living in non-traditional and poor families. Teens abused as children (see above) and who began dating early on were especially likely to engage in sexual activity. Also, youth who were worried about their friends' attitudes and perceptions of them were more likely to be sexually active. Finally, community context also explained teenage sexual activity, as community leaders and mentors helped communicate effective prevention strategies (Little and Rankin 2001).

In a more recent review of research on teen sexual activities, pregnancy, and STDs, Meade and Ickovics (2005) pointed out that an effective explanation of youth sexual behavior required integration of factors from many different levels, ranging from the individual to the broader society. These risk factors include poor education, inconsistent condom use, positive attitudes toward childbearing, and being in long-term relationships. They advocated Bronfenbrenner's (1989) Ecological Systems Theory to organize the explanations. Ecological Systems Theory emphasizes the dynamic relationship between individuals and their social environments over time, noting that factors at one level can impact those at other levels. For example, poor education increases teen pregnancy, which may in turn limit future educational/occupational endeavors. Recall from the beginning of the chapter that this was one reason teen sexual activity is especially problematic. Moreover, the Ecological Systems Theory explains how teen pregnancy results from the broader environmental factors, including poverty and cultural norms.

Sexual Identity and Coming Out

Sexual activity among heterosexual teens and young adults certainly leads to numerous complications for them as well as for the larger society. Teens who engage in such behavior may be both disliked (by parents' groups or government watchdog groups) and celebrated (by feature film and other popular culture stakeholders). However, this behavior is implicitly condoned in one important respect: it is socially approved heterosexual activity. Young people who deviate from such heterosexual behavior or identities are, on the contrary, heavily stigmatized and are believed to constitute yet another problem population.

Despite a trend toward increased acceptance of gays, lesbians, and bisexuals in our society (Enten 2007; Loftus 2001), **gay**, **lesbian**, and **bisexual** teens experience other kinds of sexual issues. While it is difficult to gauge how many gay, lesbian, and bisexual youth there are in society today, reliable sources (D'Emilio 2003; Gates 2006) estimate about 6–10 percent of the U.S. population identifies as gay, lesbian and bisexual. At least two factors make more concrete figures difficult to come by, both of which may disproportionately impact youth. First, it is difficult to define who is actually homosexual or bisexual. Most estimates are based on those who "identify" as gay, lesbian, or bisexual and such identification typically has come later in adulthood. If estimates of the homosexual and bisexual population were based simply on same-sex sexual activities, the numbers would be much higher. Second, estimates likely underrepresent the population because of the considerable social stigma of homosexuals in society. Youth are especially vulnerable to such stigma since they are dependent on adults and going through identity development and maturation. Recall the point made above about the difficulties youth face becoming sexual beings as they transition from childhood to adulthood.

Explaining Homosexuality

In general, sociologists do not subscribe to biological theories of sexuality that claim being heterosexual or gay/lesbian is a function of genes or brain composition. Sociologists believe that sexual orientation—heterosexual, bisexual, and homosexual—comes about through the socialization process. Symbolic interactionists point out that heterosexuality is often viewed as a given or a natural process because it is the established norm and it shapes so much of our lives and the institutions and practices that define our society. This is something structural functionalists call attention to, warning us that homosexuality threatens the stability of society (Kendall 2010).

Symbolic interactionists have identified several stages in accepting one's gay or lesbian identity (Weinberg, Williams, and Pryor 1994). We know today, that these steps are likely to begin in adolescence (Eliason 1996). The first stage is identity confusion—where people feel different from others and notice their attraction to the same sex. Since adolescence is fraught with identity problems in general, it is not surprising that we would find young people going through this stage during their teenage years. A second stage is establishing a gay and lesbian identity and seeking out others who are openly gay with whom to interact. This might include getting involved in gay subcultures or communities. In the past, this stage was almost exclusively experienced by adults. However, more and more teens are experiencing this stage due, perhaps, to the increased social tolerance for and visibility of gays and lesbians in society. This leads to the third stage of accepting the homosexual identity and living a life that reflects that identity and experience (Weinberg, Williams, and Pryor 1994).

Life as a Homosexual

The everyday manifestation of homosexuality plays out differently among youth and adults. There is often disagreement over how to live openly as gay and lesbian. One school of thought—**assimilation**—is consistent with the structural functionalist paradigm. It claims that homosexuals ought to focus on their sameness with heterosexuals and argue for equal access into traditional heterosexual institutions (e.g., marriage, parenting—see Elia 2003; Folgero 2008; Rimmerman 2008). A second school of thought—**queer theory**—aligns more closely with conflict theory. Queer theorists focus more on difference, i.e., the cultural uniqueness of gay lifestyle and gay identity (Rimmerman 2008), one that embraces a new way to see the world. Queer theorists are concerned with the loss of cultural uniqueness and collective identity among homosexuals from assimilation to heterosexual lifestyles.

Irrespective of the lifestyle adaptation, gay, lesbian, and bisexual teens experience an array of problems that distinguish them from their heterosexual peers. Research shows homosexual stigma, or internalized **homophobia**, negatively impacts gay, lesbian, bisexual, and transgender (GLBT) teens' mental and physical health (Wright and Perry 2006). Internalized homophobia has been linked to suicide attempts by youth struggling with sexual orientation issues (Gibson 1989; Remafedi, Farrow, and Deisher 1991). Substance abuse is also a problem for gay, lesbian, and bisexual teens. For example, Rosario et al. (1996) found relatively high levels of alcohol and illicit drug use in a sample of gay, lesbian and bisexual youth in New York City. They concluded that the stress and difficulties associated with growing up gay were the most likely cause of the elevated rates of substance use.

The relationship between internalized homophobia and mental and physical health problems (e.g., substance abuse and suicide) that Wright and Brea (2006) review can be explained by ideas from symbolic interactionism. For example, dealing with homosexual stigma and harassment from interacting with others creates stress for GLBT teens. As Chapter III points out, drugs and alcohol are often used to cope with stress, negative life experiences, and trauma. This is because their chemical properties alter perceptions (allowing people to forget their problems) and feelings (e.g., replacing depression with intoxication or euphoria). It is not surprising, therefore, that gay, lesbian, and bisexual teens would resort to substance use to quell this stress. While past research supports this point, the Wright and Brea (2006) study reaches a different conclusion: gay, lesbian and bisexual youth are actually less likely than their heterosexual peers to abuse alcohol and drugs.

As heterosexual, homosexual, and bisexual youth transition into young adults, they encounter new opportunities and situations regarding sexual activity. As young adults, they are expected to exercise increased maturity and responsibility. In the remainder of this chapter, I discuss a few issues that young adults face in expressing their sexuality and in negotiating sexual activities. I call attention to historical changes in sexual interaction and how they are related to significant problems not only for young adults, but also the wider society.

Hooking up, Date Rape, and Sexual Assault

Perhaps one of the most significant sociological developments in contemporary society has been the transition away from traditional dating to hooking up as the predominant form of courtship and sexual interaction among teens and young adults (Bogle 2008, 2009). Hooking up is defined as a physical encounter between two people with little to no expectations of further interaction (Glenn and Marquardt 2001). Hooking up can mean almost any type of interaction, from kissing to sexual intercourse. While teens hook up, the phenomenon was named for behavior among young adults, especially college students of the latter 20th and early 21st centuries.

The shift from dating to hooking up might cause alarm among **moral entrepreneurs** who have consistently campaigned against teen sexuality and advocated closely monitoring it. This is because hooking up detaches social expectations and responsibility from sexual activity. It makes sex beholden to nothing except its own pleasure (Bogle 2008). Dating and traditional courtship activities enforced a system of social control based in family obligation, i.e., intimate interaction follows the rules of family formation, via courtship and marriage and then sex (Bailey 1988), something consistent with the structural functionalist perspective. Having a new sexual script to follow—hooking up—that detaches sex from family expectations might lead to young generations not receiving traditional messages or pressure to adhere to those norms. In hooking up, people can skip the family norms and go right to sexual interaction for its own pleasure. This is something that worries conservatives and family advocates.

The detachment of sexual interaction from family expectations via **hooking up** might challenge traditional norms (a concern also with gay and lesbian sexual behaviors), but does it constitute a social problem among young people? There are a few ways that hooking up can lead to problems among youth, including those discussed in this book. First, research shows that alcohol plays a central role in facilitating hook-ups, more so than it did in the dating era (Bailey, 1988). As Chapter III notes, alcohol constitutes numerous problems on college campuses. Students understand that drinking alcohol lowers inhibitions, which helps make a hook-up possible. This might help explain the increasing role of "partying" on college campuses (Moffatt 1989; Strouse 1987).

Second, and closely related, the combination of alcohol and sexual activity, started with hooking up, may lead to **sexual assault**. Sexual assault is one of the most serious problems on college campuses and among young adults. Unlike many of the other social problems discussed in this book, sexual assault is heavily patterned by gender. Overwhelmingly, males sexually victimize females and, to a lesser extent, other males. Consider some findings from a recent **National Crime Victimization Survey** (NCVS)—the most authoritative accounting of the problem. NCVS data show that 1.6 of every 1,000 females experienced a rape or sexual assault in 2004. Most of these victims are young adult women. In fact, 16- to 24-year-old racial and ethnic minority females living in urban areas experience higher victimization rates (Catalano 2005) than any other group. Research indicates that not only is sexual assault committed mostly by males against females, but that the two usually know each other in some capacity (Bachman and Saltzman 1995; Catalano 2005; Fisher, Cullen, and Turner 2000; Tjaden and Thoennes 1998).

Explaining Sexual Assault

Research has identified many individual-level factors that help explain sexual assault. Many are consistent with symbolic interaction theory. For example, research shows a close connection between sexual assault and drug and alcohol careers (Felson and Burchfield 2004; Mohler-Kuo, Dowdall, and Koss 2004; Sherley 2005), criminal propensity and personality variables (Leonard et al. 2003; Lussier, Proulx, and LeBlanc 2005; Sherley 2005), permissive attitudes and faulty perceptions regarding sexual assault. Power concerns and hyper-masculine values among males also explain why males sexually assault females (Graham, West, and Wells 2000).

The many studies of alcohol and drug-related sexual assault victimization provide strong evidence that locations providing such substances and housing individuals who consume them are likely "**hot spots**" for sexual assault victimization. Nightclubs and bars, venues that young adults can now attend, are in business to provide alcohol-related leisure activity and their patrons attend them for these purposes. Thus, if sexual assault victimization is related to alcohol consumption, then nightclubs become a risky location for it. This point is supported by research indicating that bars and nightclubs are a leading location for sexual violence such as rape, attempted rape, and stalking (Fox and Sobol 2000; Graham and Wells 2001; Graham, West, and Wells 2000; Parks 2000). I discuss this more in the next chapter.

Conclusions

I began this chapter illustrating the contradictory ways in which youth sexuality is viewed in our society. Popular culture often celebrates many of the very youth sexual behaviors that professionals, experts, and policy makers chastise and control. While these problems are both real and, at times, overblown, they begin in childhood and can have long-term effects. This is the case with the sexual victimization of children, a problem that impacts thousands of children daily and will have long-term repercussions for many of them. We learned that parents are the most common child sexual abuse offenders, not teachers, coaches, priests, or strangers. We also learned sexually abused children are at greater risk for other youth sexual problems, e.g., premarital sex, STDs and HIV, and teen pregnancy. In Chapter III, you will read about the relationship between child abuse and substance use.

Youth sexuality is fundamentally connected to adolescent identity development, such that recognizing oneself as an independent, responsible person requires resolving who one is sexually, i.e., how will I relate to and interact with others physically, and with whom will I do so? Problems of sexual identity and sexual orientation are, consequently, tied very closely to the transition between childhood, adolescence, and young adulthood. This tension persists into young adulthood as has, in the 21st century, helped motivated new patterns of sexual interaction, like hooking up instead of traditional courtship. While we do not yet know if all of the concerns about hooking up are well-grounded, it is clear that its culture and the contexts (e.g. college campuses and urban nightlife) in which it most often takes place feature and seem to condone numerous problematic behaviors of young adults. One of the most pressing is substance use, including alcohol abuse, to which we will now turn our attention.

DISCUSSION QUESTIONS

1. To what extent do you believe hooking up will change gender relations and equality between men and women?
2. How would increased tolerance of homosexuality in society alter the coming out process for teens? Explain any race, class or gender differences you might anticipate.

III: Substance Abuse

Introduction

It started with a random text message sent in error to deputy policewoman and D.A.R.E. officer Kari Scherer. A 16-year-old boy in Portage County, Ohio was looking for some killer weed (i.e., marijuana) when he accidentally sent the message to Officer Scherer, who then set up a sting to nab the boy's drug dealing network. Participating Sheriff Doaks commented that, "People think that they can make quick money, kids are enticed by that at times and there's serious consequences to it and we hope that he's learned a lesson from it" (Ziemba, 2010).

While some find the Portage County text messaging case humorous, others see it as evidence that youth substance abuse problems are running out of control in modern society. News reports like this one are common, and government officials inform us daily about a wide variety of youth substance abuse problems: underage drinking and motor vehicle accidents, alcohol poisoning and drug overdose deaths, drug dealing by youth gangs, alcohol-related violence and sexual assault, adolescent drug use and experimentation, non-medical use of prescription painkillers and ADHD medications, and drug addiction associated with adolescent anxiety and identity development.

Alarming figures are tossed about in an attempt to warrant increased attention and action toward these substance abuse problems. Whether these figures are used to construct a moral panic or pursue a political agenda, few dispute that they cannot be ignored. Consider the case of underage drinking. According to a report by the National Academy of Sciences (NAS 2003), underage drinking costs society a whopping $53 billion a year. These figures are not only significant, they clearly indicate how youth social problems are interconnected, including to those problems addressed in this book. The breakdown of the $53 billion by the National Academy of Sciences (NAS 2003) is shown in Table 3.1.

As you can see, underage drinking by teens not only led to other substance abuse problems (i.e., fetal alcohol syndrome, alcohol poisoning and treatment), but also to violence and suicide. While these statistics are troubling, even more problematic is the number of youth alcohol-related injuries and fatalities. Teenagers and young adults between 15 and 24 years of age have the highest death rates for motor vehicle traffic-related injuries. In fact, 2005 data show that about one-fifth of 16- to 20-year-old drivers killed in traffic-related crashes were intoxicated (NHTSA 2005).

Table 3.1 Breakdown of Underage Drinking Costs to Society

Issue	Cost
Violent crime	$29,368,000,000
Traffic crashes	$19,452,000,000
Burns	$189,000,000
Drowning	$426,000,000
Suicide attempts	$1,512,000,000
Fetal alcohol syndrome	$493,000,000
Alcohol poisonings	$340,000,000
Treatment	$1,008,000,000
TOTAL	**$52,788,000,000**

The problems for society from teen alcohol abuse are not restricted to driving while intoxicated. In general, drinking by teens and young adults constitutes significant health care harms. For example, The National Hospital Ambulatory Medical Care Survey (NHAMCS) collects annual data on alcohol-related visits to hospital emergency departments (EDs). The survey counted more than 230,000 alcohol-related visits per year among 14- to 20-year-olds between 2002 and 2004, which is about 2 percent of all adolescent emergency department visits.

From these surveys, we once again learn that social problems are patterned and not evenly distributed among the U.S. population. In other words, some youth are more likely to engage in underage drinking and suffer from traffic-related death and injury or alcohol poisoning and overdose than others. For example, the NHAMCS shows that alcohol-related ED visits are higher for males than females and that the problem for males remains stable through early adulthood before it tapers off. Also interesting is that black 11th and 12th grade students were less likely to drive after drinking than non-Hispanic white or Hispanic students.

In this chapter, I discuss some of the substance abuse problems teens and young adults experience in the 21st century. Consistent with this book's objectives, I focus on how these matters are socially constructed as problems society must address, how they are patterned by social group and context, and how they are connected to other social problems, including sexuality and suicide. For example, as mentioned in the previous chapter, alcohol-related sexual assault is one of the leading problems on college campuses and in bars and nightclubs. Research has also established strong ties between childhood sexual abuse victimization and later substance abuse problems. Finally, research on adolescent sexuality has found that the coming out process puts gay and lesbian youth at high risk for substance abuse problems—and suicide, for that matter (see Chapter IV). While there are many things to consider in explaining sexuality problems and suicide, these research findings illustrate that youth social problems are interconnected.

The Extent of Drug and Alcohol Use and Abuse among Youth and Young Adults

The level, amount, and frequency of information collected on something is a very good indicator of how much concern a society, and its public and private institutions, have about it. Consider the mountain of data collected annually on the extent of drug and alcohol use and abuse among young people in our society. The U.S. federal government funds numerous large surveys to collect information about all kinds of substance use and abuse annually. There is the **Monitoring the Future study**, funded by the National Institute on Drug Abuse (NIDA), which collects substance use data on high school kids. The CDC-sponsored Youth Risk Behavior Survey (YRBS) collects not only substance abuse data on youth, but also on a variety of other behaviors it deems "risky." The **National Longitudinal Study of Adolescent Health Survey**, i.e, AddHealth, surveys the health conditions of young people, including their drug and alcohol consumption and health-related complications. If these didn't teach us enough, there is also the premier federal substance abuse monitoring effort—the **National Survey on Drug Use and Health** (NSDUH) —which collects annual data on all sorts of substance use and abuse behaviors and problems among Americans between the ages of 12 and 94. Every year, researchers and policy makers pore over the latest findings from these surveys to define youth substance use problems. The data are used to bolster or criticize politicians or political initiatives.

What do all of these data on substance use tell us about the prevalence and seriousness of drug and alcohol use among teens and young adults? At a minimum, we learn that drug and alcohol use are patterned by social group in our society and that certain rates fluctuate over time for all groups—suggesting that substance use patterns are influenced by historical events, environmental factors, and social trends. Evidence for this can be found in a recent NSDUH. The 2008 survey has concluded that substance use and abuse among youth (i.e., 12- to 17-year-olds) has, in general, declined slightly during the first decade of the 21st century (NSDUH 2008). For example, in 2002 about 18 percent of teens drank alcohol in the past month, while 16 percent reported doing so in 2007. Past month illicit drug use also dropped: from about 12 percent in 2002 to about 10 percent in 2007. The report even finds that rates of drug dependence among teens have also dropped between 2002 and 2007: from 5.6 to 4.3 percent respectively. Teens' dependence on alcohol, however, remained stable during the same time period. The same report, however, notes a slight rise in a new form of drug use that was not much of an issue, or at least not identified as one, in the 20th century: non-medical use of prescription drugs.

The change in illicit drug use is largely due to a decline in marijuana use. This is an interesting observation since marijuana has been the most commonly used drug across age group for decades (Courtwright 2001; Johnston, O'Malley, and Bachman 2003) and is the only illegal drug to be made available for sale in 13 states for 'medical' conditions. In California where laws on marijuana are the least restrictive, marijuana use rates for both youth and adults exceed national averages. For example, data from NORML California (2009) show that nearly 50 percent of all high school students in California smoked marijuana before graduation and 25 percent of them used marijuana in the past month. The most recent student survey in California claims, "Since 2003, use in the past six months has remained stable at 7% in 7th grade, 20% in 9th and 31% in 11th grade" (NORML California, 2009). While these rates have declined since marijuana was made available for medical use in 1996 by Proposition 215, they still show that teen marijuana use is higher in California than in the nation as a whole.

Is Youth Substance Use a Social Problem?

From these substance use surveys, we learn that young people use and abuse substances other than marijuana and alcohol with relative frequency and intensity. Yet, we may wonder if they warrant designation as social problems and justify the resources society spends on them? Experts and other stakeholders, as well as everyday citizens, likely have an opinion about this matter. Two of the most persistent patterns in substance use may offer support for both sides of the debate.

First, many studies (using these data sets and others) have concluded that teen substance use progresses onto other, "harder" drugs (e.g., cocaine and heroin) after marijuana use. Research consistently shows that some teens who use alcohol and marijuana will likely progress onto drugs like cocaine and heroin later in life. Researchers and policy makers call this the **gateway hypothesis** and it is a primary concern about teen substance use because so-called harder drugs like cocaine and heroin feature harsh psychological and physiological withdrawal and high risk of dependence and involvement in illegal activities. According to the 2008 NSDUH survey, for example, about 16.5 percent of young adults reported being current users of marijuana in 2008, while 5.9 percent used psychotherapeutics for non-medical reasons, 1.7 percent used hallucinogens and 2.6 percent cocaine. Gateway proponents (Kandel 2003; Kandel et al. 2006) argue that if left unchecked, teen alcohol and marijuana use could lead to the abuse of harder drugs and enmeshment in the types of deviant careers that symbolic interaction theorists describe. Additional social problems, like crime and unemployment, are likely to follow. The diversification of drug use over time and manifestation of related social problems justify, many believe, the classification of youth alcohol and marijuana use as a social problem.

An opposing position is that youth alcohol and marijuana use is more a **rite of passage** rather than a full-scale social problem demanding societal attention. Those who take this position look at some of the same data and see that the majority of young people who use marijuana or alcohol do not progress onto harder drugs (Golub, Johnson, and Dunlap 2005). More importantly, they point out that youth marijuana and alcohol use peak in late adolescence and early adulthood but decline sharply afterwards.

For example, the NSDUH (2009) shows that about 9.3 percent of teens between 12 and 17 years of age were current users of illicit drugs in 2008. Broken down by drug, the NSDUH reports that 6.7 percent used marijuana, 2.9 percent engaged in non-medical use of prescription-type psychotherapeutics, 1.1 percent used inhalants, 1.0 percent used hallucinogens, and 0.4 percent used cocaine. These rates increase as teens become young adults. For example, the NSDUH shows that the 2008 rates of current drug use were higher (19.6 percent), across all types of drugs, than for teens aged 12 and 17 (9.3 percent). The good news is that rates for 18- to 25-year-olds were also higher than those for adults aged 26 or older, suggesting that drug use declines after peaking in early adulthood.

This so-called age-curve in substance use, many argue, is a normal part of growing up in the U.S. (Golub, Johnson, and Labouvie 2000). Best not to panic over youth substance use and chastise them too harshly because most will grow out of it by the time they begin working fulltime or move into their late 20s and early 30s. Many symbolic interactionists took this position because, as indicated in Chapter I, formal labeling of young people (e.g., arrests for substance use) could lead to a stigma, a self-fulfilling prophecy and a career in deviance. Instead, they argued that issues like youth substance use should be dealt with by prevention and education programs.

Demographic Patterns in Drug Use

Perhaps one of the most interesting historical developments in substance use is the convergence between males' and females' substance use rates. Whereas male drug use once outpaced females considerably, data in the 21st century consistently reveal more parity between them. For example, the 2008 NSDUH shows that male and female 12- to 17-year-olds had similar rates of current illicit drug use overall (9.5 percent for males and 9.1 percent for females) and for drugs like cocaine (0.5 and 0.3 percent, respectively), hallucinogens (1.1 and 0.8 percent), and inhalants (1.1 percent for both). Marijuana and non-medical use of prescription drugs turned up differences between males and females. Current marijuana use was more prevalent among males (7.3 percent) than females (6.0 percent), while non-medical use of psychotherapeutic drugs among was more prevalent among females (3.3 percent) than males (2.5 percent), as was non-medical use of painrelievers (2.6 and 2.0 percent, respectively).

There are also differences in youth drug use by racial group. According to the NSDUH (2007), the highest rates of any illicit drug use are found among mixed race, Native American, and Hawaiian/Pacific Island youth: 12.7, 12.6, and 12.5 respectively in 2004 and 2005. These three racial groups also reported higher rates of marijuana and non-medical use of prescription drugs than did white, black, Hispanic and Asian youth.

Over the years, there have been many stories circulating in popular culture about sinister older drug dealers preying on the vulnerabilities of youth. In the 1950s, they were famously portrayed in the film *Reefer Madness*. More recently, stories about candy-colored, packaged and flavored marijuana and methamphetamine prompted the U.S. Senate Judiciary Committee, at the urging of Senator Diana Feinstein, to pass a new measure to punish predatory drug dealers. Senator Feinstein stated:

> This bill sends a strong and clear message to drug dealers—if you target our children by peddling candy-flavored drugs, there will be a heavy price to pay. The legislation increases criminal penalties for anyone who markets candy–flavored drugs in an effort to hook our young people.
>
> (www.feinstein.senate.gov)

The narrative used by Feinstein and her senate colleagues tells of adult drug dealers lurking about on school grounds or in other youth-oriented spaces luring young people into experimentation with drugs. Such predatory behavior is claimed to ensnare youth into careers in drugs and deviance over the lifecourse.

While often effective in raising attention to youth problems, research shows that such narratives and claims are more fictional than real, leading some sociologists to call them **urban legends**. By looking no further than to the federal government's own reports, we can find evidence to dispel this narrative. According to a 2004 report by the NSDUH, most youth get their marijuana free and from a friend. They aren't manipulated into giving their money away to an anonymous drug dealer. Females are especially likely to get their marijuana free from a friend. They also are more likely than males to share their marijuana with others. Youth most often obtain their marijuana from inside a home, apartment or dorm, not in a public space such as a playground or school. However, when kids do buy marijuana—not get it for free—they are more likely to buy it in a public location. About 20 percent of teens who pay for their pot say they got it on a public street (NSDUH 2004). Yet, very few of them buy it at a school or schoolyard playspace. This indicates that schools are not a frequent spot for illegal drug dealing, contrary to some press reports and public sentiment.

Despite all of this information on illegal drug use, alcohol use and abuse remain far more problematic since teens and young adults drink alcohol with far greater frequency, intensity, and complication than they use all illegal drugs combined. Data across the surveys mentioned above consistently show that youth alcohol use is the primary substance abuse problem of that demographic.

Alcohol Use and Demographic Patterns

Let's compare the alcohol rates with the illegal drug rates. According to the NSDUH (2009a), 14.6 percent of teens aged 12–17 were current users of alcohol. Compare that with 9.3 percent for drug use. Keep in mind that any alcohol use under 21 years of age is illegal behavior.

Young people do not only drink alcohol more often than they use illegal drugs, they also consume more of it, often surpassing their older counterparts. Consider what the data show about **binge drinking** (i.e., five or more drinks in any one occasion) and **heavy drinking** (binge drinking on five or more days per week) by youth and young adults. According to the NSDUH (2009a), about 20 percent of all people surveyed (i.e., 12- to 94-year-olds) reported binge drinking at least once in the past month. Rates of both binge and heavy drinking steadily increase from the teen years into young adulthood. They begin declining after 30 years of age. For example, 2008 NSDUH data show rates of binge drinking at 1.5 percent for 12- or 13-year-olds, 6.9 percent for 14- or 15-year-olds, 17.2 percent for 16- or 17-year-olds, 33.7 percent for 18- to 20-year-olds, and a whopping 46 percent for 21- to 25-year-olds. Binge drinking rates fall considerably afterwards. Such levels of alcohol use among young people cause numerous other social problems, including alcohol-related car accidents and to overdose on alcohol, and suffer acute alcohol poisoning from drinking games.

Differences by socio-demographic group escalate when we look at binge and heavy drinking. To begin, males are more likely to be binge and heavy drinkers than females. Consequently, it is not surprising then that males aged 12–20 had higher rates of alcohol use disorder than females (10.3 percent to 8.5 percent respectively). The rate of past year alcohol use disorder among persons aged 12–20 was higher for American Indians or Alaska Natives (14.9 percent) than for whites (10.9 percent), blacks (4.6 percent), Hispanics (8.7 percent), and Asians (4.9 percent). One in eight Native Hawaiians or Other Pacific Islanders (12.7 percent) met the criteria for an alcohol use disorder.

Explaining Youth Substance Use

How can we explain these patterns of substance use among teens and young adults? As indicated in Chapter I, there are micro-level theories that focus on individual reasons and more macro-level theories that focus on structural or environmental causes. Many of the researchers who are involved with data collection in the above mentioned surveys focus on individual motivations. For example, Terry-McElrath et al. (2009: 678) published a major paper that summarized reasons for youth substance abuse between 1976 and 2005 from the Monitoring the Future Study of high school kids. They concluded that teens were motivated to use drugs and alcohol for four main reasons: (1) enhancement (to enhance positive mood; internally based); (2) social (related to obtaining social rewards; externally based); (3) coping (to decrease negative emotions; internally based), and (4) conformity (to avoid social rejection; externally based).

The researchers also concluded that motivations for individual drug use were patterned by gender, race, and ethnicity, further supporting the objectives of this book. For example, females were more likely to use drugs for reasons related to coping with negative feelings (such as anger, frustration, or other problems) or for compulsive behaviors (such as self-perceived addiction). In contrast, males were more likely to report social and recreational reasons for use. Males were also more likely to use certain drugs to enhance the effects of others, thus contributing to cross-dependency and other complications. Terry-McElrath et al.'s (2009) study also shows race-related differences in youth drug use motivations. White youth, for example, most often reported using drugs for social and recreational reasons whereas Black youth more often reported using them to "get through the day." Hispanics reported using drugs to deal with dependency issues.

While this study reveals some very useful information on the motivations behind youth drug use across social group, many other studies point to more structural or environmental reasons as well. In the next two sections, I review some of these more macro-level explanations for youth substance use and related problems: family substance abuse and the search for social identity. Doing so will further support the importance of the book's three objectives.

Family Substance Abuse, Child Abuse, and Youth Risk

Starting at home and within the family, teens are troubled by drugs and alcohol in multiple ways. Children and teens are often dependent on parents who use and abuse drugs and alcohol. Recent studies show that about 9 percent of U.S. children (6 million) live with at least one parent who abuses alcohol or other drugs. These substance-abusing parents pose multiple problems for young people, including increased risk for abuse and neglect. Research shows children of substance-abusing parents are more likely to experience physical, sexual, or emotional abuse or neglect than children raised in non-drug abusing households (Dube et al. 2001).

The impact of substance abuse on young people can begin before birth. Drug-abusing pregnant women pose numerous risks to the unborn (i.e., **teratogenic effects**), including birth defects and impaired brain and motor development. The most widely documented teratogenic effects—long-term and short-term—stem from alcohol use. A mother's alcohol use during pregnancy can cause growth retardation, damage to the central nervous system, facial abnormalities, and mental retardation (Robbins 2007). Yet, alcohol's impact on children seldom receives the level of scrutiny by the media and policy makers as do illegal drugs. As a result, the general public is more likely to think illegal drug use by parents is more dangerous to unborn children than alcohol use. This is another example of how social problems are socially constructed.

During the 1980s and 1990s the U.S. experienced a considerable crack cocaine problem (Johnson, Golub, and Fagan 1995). A moral panic about drug-exposed babies and impaired brain development of a generation of young people surfaced and created considerable public alarm (Lester, Andreozzi, and Appiah 2004). While research has shown there are some important short-term impacts from a parent's cocaine use on unborn infants (Frank et al. 2001; Singer et al. 2002), it has largely dismissed concerns about long-term developmental consequences from crack cocaine-abusing mothers (Provine 2007; Ritchie 2002).

While teratogenic effects from alcohol and other substance abuse are problematic, the bigger risk to young people may be from how substance-abusing parents treat their children. Research shows a consistent and strong connection between parents' substance abuse and child abuse and neglect (Dube et al. 2001; Kelleher et al. 1994). Nearly 40 percent of documented child maltreatment cases involve the use of alcohol or drugs by parents and guardians. In fact, Child Protective Service agencies have estimated that substance abuse is a factor in a majority of the cases it handles (Child Welfare website n.d.).

Substance-abusing parents neglect their children by often spending money on drugs and alcohol instead of food, clothing, and shelter. Parents who abuse alcohol and drugs are also less likely to maintain steady employment and health insurance. Also, substance-abusing parents tend to be detached from their kids and unable to provide for their physical and emotional care. Drug and alcohol use consume people's time, rendering them unable to prioritize daily tasks and relationships. Also, many substance-abusing parents engage in illegal activities and, consequently, end up in the criminal justice system. Researchers estimated that in the early 21st century, approximately 1.5 million children under age 18 had parents in prison (Richie 2002). Most had a father in prison, but for nearly 125,000 of these children their mother was incarcerated as well. All of these things place children at increased risk for malnutrition, illness, accidental injury, school failure, and delinquency. Substance-abusing behaviors of parents may expose their children to the deviant behaviors of dangerous people. Physical and sexual abuse victimization can result, thus illustrating the connection between substance abuse problems and those related to sex and sexuality.

Finally, when young people grow up in households with substance-abusing parents and other adults, they are more likely to become substance abusers themselves. Sociologists call this the **family transmission thesis** and find that children whose parents drink and use drugs are, themselves, more likely to drink and use drugs in adolescence and adulthood. Young people are also more likely to use alcohol and drugs if they have older siblings who do (Jones and Jones 2000).

This family transmission thesis is closely tied to an important symbolic interaction or social process theory that has been popular in explaining youth substance abuse. Social learning theory maintains that youth learn about the properties and effects of drugs and alcohol from their family members. They also learn how to use substances (i.e., smoke, inject, snort). Most importantly, perhaps, parents and siblings convey beliefs and attitudes about the value of altering mental states (e.g., sobriety, arousal, sedation, hallucinatory states) through drugs and alcohol.

The Search for Identity: Discovery and Coping via Drugs

Certainly, family drug use plays an important role in explaining the substance abuse problems of youth; however, not all teens who abuse drugs and alcohol come from drug-abusing families. This underscores the need for other theories. Moreover, it highlights the point that sociologists seldom explain social problems as emanating from one cause. Multiple causes are typically identified and they exist at different levels of analysis, a point made in Chapter I.

Today, we know that drugs and alcohol serve many functions to those that use them. At the micro level, research has taught us that teens and young adults also use drugs and alcohol to cope with life events and to handle identity issues. Childhood trauma and alienation, as well as the uncertainties associated with becoming an independent person, force some youth and young adults to quell their feelings and stress with drugs and alcohol (Anderson 1998a). Drugs and alcohol work to anesthetize negative feelings (e.g., especially sedatives and narcotics) and can fool people into thinking they are someone different while high or intoxicated or at least have traits that are desired (Anderson 1993, 1994). For example, Kaplan, Martin, and Robbins (1984, 1986) established that drug use helps adolescents resolve problems with self-derogation—negative feelings about the self—while Anderson (1994, 1998a, 2005) added that it serves to both insulate young people from alienating experiences and trauma in childhood and to help them create new identities that are socially approved by important others, e.g., drug-using peers.

At a macro level, drugs and illegal drug activities provide both identity and material opportunities that are attractive to youth, especially those hailing from disadvantaged backgrounds in impoverished locations. As mentioned in Chapter I, structural functionalist and conflict theorists have explained how macro-level factors shape individual opportunities and foster the motivations to engage in deviant behaviors such as drug use, drug-dealing. etc.

One structural theory to pay particular attention to this matter is social reproduction theory. Recall from Chapter I Bourdieu's (1977) claim that while schools promised youth upward mobility in society, they instead reproduced inequality, discouraging improvements in class position, by channeling working-class and poor kids into coursework targeting semi-skilled employment and upper-class kids into academic coursework needed for college. Inequality in society was, consequently, maintained.

Scholars from this approach point out that people acquire at birth and accumulate throughout their lives unequal shares of several types of capital (social, financial, human, and personal) that affect their life chances. Financial capital, i.e., material forms of wealth such as money, credit, investment, and assets—the kind Marx (1995, Marx and Engels 1992) discussed, are what most think of when assessing inequality. Parents with greater financial assets can simply pay for better opportunities for their children. Poorer parents cannot provide these things. Thus their children are dependent on social supports (e.g., college tuition, loan programs) from the state. Absent such financial capital and the opportunities it provides, lower-class children may result to alternative, illegal means to achieve the same things, e.g., drug dealing, which could eventually lead to substance abuse. This was also a major premise of Merton's (1968) structural strain theory.

However, social reproduction theorists pointed to other types of capital that widened the inequality/goal attainment gap not previously discussed by structural functionalists or conflict theorists. One type was human capital, i.e., degrees, education, skills, training, and experience, which is required so that individuals can provide for themselves and others and alter their class position. However, lower-class youth lack another critical form of capital possessed by the middle and upper classes—social capital, which are one's ties or connections to others who can do things for you or provide special treatment and access. Research (McCarthy and Hagan 2001) shows that social capital (e.g., networking and access to powerful others) is critically important in securing valuable resources, including college admission and employment. It also shows such capital is not evenly distributed by class, race, ethnicity, or gender.

Numerous studies have used social reproduction theory to explain illegal drug activities by young people. Studies by Venkatesh (2000) and Venkatesh and Levitt (2000) on criminal and drug gangs in Chicago, Bourgois (1996) and Maher (1996) in New York city, MacLeod's (1987) account of high school youth in the Midwest, and Jacobs (1999) and Miller's (2000) work in St. Louis all lend support to the social reproduction theory claims that inequities in social, financial, and human capital serve as a form of alienation that marginalizes people from conventional society and put them at increased risk for illegal drug activities.

McCarthy and Hagan (2001) introduced **personal capital**—a desire for wealth, risk-taking propensity, willingness to cooperate, and competence—to further elaborate these ideas. Selling drugs and/or participation in criminal markets requires some of the same personality traits or identity characteristics required for success in corporate America. Hagan and colleagues maintain, however, that the utilization of personal capital for successful illicit gain fosters strong disincentives for conventional activities. Anderson (2005) also makes this point, showing that competence in negotiating the illicit drug world instills a kind of validation that participants perceive they cannot find in a punitive society that stigmatizes them. 'Criminal success' unfortunately cements enmeshment in deviant activities. Alas, it is short-lived. Continued illegal activities increase the likelihood of arrest and incarceration, which conversely further damages any type of capital one possesses.

Prescription Drug Abuse: Teens and College Students

According to the NSDUH (2009b), non-medical use of **prescription painrelievers** is now the second most common type of illicit drug use in our country. What authorities mean by this is that drugs prescribed to certain patients by medical doctors to treat their health problems are being used, instead, by others for recreational purposes or to simply get high. This amounts to illegal behavior since prescribed medications are controlled by the federal government.

For many years, cocaine followed marijuana as the most frequently used illegal drug among adults while hallucinogens did so for youth (Kandel et al. 2006; Johnston, O'Malley, and Bachman 2003). The movement of non-medical use of prescription painkillers into second place accounts for a dramatic historical development and says a lot about the 21st century in which we live. For our purposes here, it could mean that youth nonmedical substance abuse may take on different forms and explanations, produce a new set of consequences, and require unique solutions.

Let's take a look at the form non-medical drug use takes among young people. The most authoritative source on this is, once again, the NSDUH sponsored by the federal government. According to the NSDUH, the most commonly abuse psychotherapeutic drugs are opiates, i.e., drugs made from the poppy plant, including the brand names Oxycontin, Percocet, and Darvon. The Drug Enforcement Administration (DEA) believes that these drugs are abused for their euphoric effects, something that has been widely known about the opiates for a long period of time (Courtwright, 2001). What is new, of course, is that people are using legal opiate-based medications for some of the same reasons that others used heroin: to get high. Even more compelling is that most of the non-medical users of prescription painkillers, tranquilizers, and sedatives are young adults, aged 18–25. Teenagers (12–17 years old) also use these drugs at high rates (NSDUH 2009b).

While prescription stimulants like Adderall, Ritalin and Focalin (drugs used to treat ADHD) are abused to a much lesser extent, they are favored by the young and have become recently newsworthy. A familiar pattern rears its head: a youth behavior, i.e., non-medical use of prescription stimulants, is both condemned and celebrated. Consider a recent *60 Minutes* exposé on Adderall and Focalin use on college campuses (http://www.cbsnews.com/stories/2010/04/22/60minutes). In an April 2010 story, Katie Couric reports that as many as 50–60 percent of students use these drugs to boost their brain power for their college exams and assignments. Couric convenes experts who both advocate this behavior (to produce a smarter generation of U.S. competitors) and admonish it (i.e., substance abuse experts who warn of addiction to prescribed stimulants). This example illustrates the contradictions in defining youth social problems in modern society.

The diversion of legally controlled substances for non-medical consumption troubles anti-drug stakeholders. Yet, most concede that it doesn't seem to be connected to crime in the way that illicit drug use is. The DEA reports that diverted controlled substances are generally distributed by individuals, among friends and family, and through rogue Internet pharmacies. They seldom follow the street-level distribution models of heroin, cocaine, marijuana, and methamphetamine, featuring drug trafficking organizations

(DTOs) and criminal groups engaged in violence. Yet, non-medical prescription drug use imposes unwanted costs for society. The DEA estimates that it has increased violent and property crime across the U.S. and costs medical insurance companies (public and private) about $73 billion a year (Drug Enforcement Administration 2010).

Alcohol Abuse on Campus and in Bars and Nightclubs

In contemporary society, cities are thriving entertainment sites where youth and young adults interact, especially in bars and nightclubs (Bennett 2001; Chatterton and Hollands 2002; Grazian 2009). The phenomenon has brought renewed resources (in terms of businesses, tourism, and service sector employment) to American cities. However, in addition to the socio-economic benefits, the growth of a nightclub-centered leisure industry has also resulted in a number of social problems that disproportionately impact teens and young adults.

Currently, media accounts suggest that nightclub events might be hot spots of deviance, characterized by alcohol use abuse, illicit drug selling and using, weapons offenses, and physical and sexual assault. News reports from New York (Berkey-Gerard 2001) cited death, overdose, violence, and murder at nightclubs. In addition, Holmberg (2001) claims that drug using and selling takes place at most nightclubs and restaurants catering to young adults in major U.S. cities. This phenomenon also exists abroad, in nations such as England, which also has a thriving youth–oriented leisure economy. Chatterton and Hollands (2002: 102) have noted that "mainstream nightlife culture continues to be awash on a sea of alcohol, with heavy circuit drinking, vandalism, and violence still commonplace."

Nightclubs and bars have come under scrutiny by local, state, and federal authorities as being noisy, socially disruptive breeding grounds for drug use and sales, as well as sites conducive to violent crime, such as sexual and physical assault (Mosler 2001; U.S. Senate Subcommittee on Juvenile Justice 1994; Valdez 2002). As such, activities occurring at nightclub events have the potential to impact both local economies and the criminal justice system.

Recently, Anderson et al. (2007) conducted an **ethnographic study** of young adults' clubbing activities in Philadelphia. They uncovered numerous types of social problems, including illegal drug use, illegal drug sales, property crime, vandalism, physical assault, and sexual assault and harassment. Other research in the U.S. (Graham and Wells 2003; Graham, West, and Wells 2000; Graham et al. 2006; Grazian 2009) and elsewhere (Hadfield 2006; Hobbs, Hadfield, and Lister 2003) has made similar discoveries.

This body of scholarship finds that over-consumption of alcohol is the norm for young adults who socialize in public bars and nightclubs. Rampant binge drinking is common among them and is often aided by a club or bar's alcohol promotions and related gimmicks (Hadfield 2006; Measham, Aldridge, and Parker 2001). Males in both club scenes reported consuming far greater amounts of alcohol than females. Excessive drinking typically resulted in more sexually related problems for women and more aggressive, physical confrontations for men. This highlights the salience of this book's objective on the interconnections among youth-oriented problems relating to sexuality, substance use, and suicide. In fact, research has found that alcohol sales at bars and clubs are associated with an increased likelihood that attendees will commit alcohol-related offenses, and that physical and sexual assault are among the most common (Buddie and Parks 2003; Hobbs, Hadfield, and Lister 2003; Leonard, Collins, and Quigley 2003). Bars and nightclubs are also leading locations for rape, attempted rape, and other forms of sexual assault and harassment (Buddie and Parks 2003; Fox and Sobol 2000).

While alcohol-related problems may be expected in bars and nightclubs, research shows drug use complications are present as well. For example, Anderson and colleagues (2007, 2009b) found considerable illegal drug use by young adults during clubbing activities. Even though most were current users of marijuana, they seldom experienced aggression or sexual problems as was reported with alcohol. Cocaine and ecstasy use are also common in nightclubs and bars, but not as common as marijuana and alcohol use.

Anderson et al.'s (2007) respondents also reported seeing illegal drugs sold at clubs and bars, mostly by 20-something males. The researchers found more violent types of deviance in clubs and bars as well, including minor physical assault (mostly fights with punching, kicking and biting) and a smaller amount of major assault (stabbings and gunshot wounds). Much of the physical assault was committed by males and concerned women or small personal affronts. Female clubbers reported being at high risk of sexual assault in nightclubs. Verbal abuse was the most common form of harassment Anderson et al. (2007) found. This typically involved a man calling a woman a "bitch or whore" after she turned down his dancing request or sexual advance. Nearly all of the female respondents reported unwanted groping or fondling by men. Although most of these accounts did not escalate to more serious assault, in some instances the groping became more violent. Female respondents reported that more serious forms of victimization (e.g., rape, attempted rape, and stalking) involved "friends" of clubbing buddies or males they knew from clubbing. They experienced less serious forms (e.g., groping, verbal harassment) from random male clubbers.

Conclusions

Our society cares an awful lot about young people's consumption of alcohol and other mood-altering substances. We can measure this by the mountains of annual data collected by federal agencies and the researchers they fund. From these numerous costly surveys, we learn some pretty compelling things, most of which are historically consistent, mixed with a few that are novel to the 21st century. First, alcohol is the most frequently and heavily used mood-altering substance by teens and young adults and it leads to more social, public health, and financial problems than any other mood-altering substance. Second, marijuana is the most commonly used illicit drug and that has remained the case for a very long time in our society. Most teens have tried marijuana and many are current users. Yet, only a few of them progress onto the harder drugs, such as cocaine and heroin, and engage in serious crime. However, for these few, early marijuana use leads to harder drugs, addiction and crime because drug use, abuse, and dependence are tied to identity needs, cultural norms, social opportunities, and a whole host of environmental factors that make drugs and the deviant lifestyle surrounding it both appealing and necessary to youth.

As teens mature into young adults, they encounter other issues with substances. Some of these, like the non-medical use of prescribed drugs, are new trends and time will tell us more about their consequences on society. In the mean time, we learned here that substance use is especially problematic for young adults when they are engaged in leisure activities outside of the home in places like bars and nightclubs. There, it is mostly the over-consumption and glorification of alcohol use—like in the film *Superbad* and so many others—that leads to rape, stalking and harassment, and physical assault.

Suicide is yet another area in which the substance abuse behaviors of teens and young adults are problematic. We turn our attention to it now, beginning with some recent stories of teen suicide and how widespread it is in our society.

DISCUSSION QUESTIONS

1. How will the gateway theory of substance use be impacted by more states making marijuana medically available to their residents?
2. How would sociologists study the influence of student culture on binge drinking and sexual assault on college campuses? Would their methods differ if studying these behaviors among different groups in other locations? How?

IV: Suicide

DOCTOR: What are you doing here, honey?
   You're not even old enough to know how bad life gets.
CECILIA: Obviously, doctor, you've never been a 13-year-old girl.
(Passage from the 1999 feature film The Virgin Suicides)

Introduction

In 2006, Megan Meier, a 13-year-old girl from Dardenne Prairie County, Missouri, committed suicide after being bullied by a fictitious male teenager on MySpace.com (Harvey 2008). Lori Drew, the 49-year-old mother of a teenage girl Megan knew, created a fictitious teenage boy identity and taunted Megan via MySpace, AOL Messenger and other computer-based communication outlets. The case raised national attention and Congressional action to what many believed was a new social problem: **cyber-bullying**. Does cyber-bullying constitute a new social problem? And to what extent does it exacerbate suicide among our nation's youth, the subject of this chapter?

At first glance, cyber-bullying seems widespread and has considerable consequences. According to National Crime Prevention Council, cyber-bullying is "when the Internet, cell phones or other devices are used to send or post text or images intended to hurt or embarrass another person" (www.ncpc.org). A whopping 40 percent of all kids surveyed reported being bullied online or in chat rooms, although girls were at higher risk for the harassment. Young people report being made to feel "threatened, embarrassed or uncomfortable" from cyber-bullying. Still, is cyber-bullying a new cause of suicide? How are the two connected? Megan's case provides some answers to these questions and another glimpse into how sociologists look at social problems like suicide and the people and groups it impacts.

Megan's death supports at least three long-standing scientific observations about teen suicide. First, research (Behman, Kliegmann, and Arvin 1996; CDC 2007; Yoder, Hoyt, and Whitbeck 1998) shows low self-esteem, depression, and **suicide ideation** are common among young suicide victims in our society. Megan Meier was an overweight teen who suffered from low self-esteem, a deficit common to adolescents during identity development (see Chapter II). She also had a history of depression and ADHD, had previously discussed suicide (i.e., suicide ideation) and had been treated by a psychiatrist since she was three years old. In this sense, then, Megan's death is tragic, but not unique. She was a depressed teen struggling to feel good about whom she was.

Second, the proliferation of psychotherapeutic drugs in our society has been linked to suicide and suicide ideation (Markowitz and Cuellar 2007). Given this, could the medications Megan was prescribed throughout her life (i.e., anti-depressants, ADHD and anti-psychotic pills), not cyber-bullying, explain her death? While some argue that such medications are a new culprit of suicide, evidence to date is mixed. For example, the Food and Drug Administration ordered all manufacturers of anti-depressants in 2004 to place a 'black box' warning on their medications warning of an increased risk of pediatric suicide. Yet, the relationship between psychotherapeutic medications and teen suicide was not clear-cut (Jureidini 2004). Recall Chapter III mentioned other notable consequences from young people's use of prescribed medications.

Finally, Megan was a girl troubled by her appearance and one who derived personal worth from male attention. Feminists, sociologists and psychologists have consistently argued that such gender-related socialization processes take a toll on young girls (Bassoff and Glass 1982). This highlights the connection between gender, adolescent identity development, and sexuality. Given all of these explanations, could it be that the MySpace and AOL Messenger attacks Megan received were simply a trigger that sent an already vulnerable girl over the edge? Whatever the explanation, it seems as though being a 13-year-old girl, articulated eloquently by Cecilia's quote in the *Virgin Suicides*, captures the angst associated with adolescence that leads so many girls like Megan Meier, and even her male peers more so, to end their lives.

The purpose of this chapter is to review what we know about suicide among young people in our society, focusing on the extent of the problem, patterns among social groups, and connections to youth sexuality and substance use. Our discussion remains focused on youth social problems as both socially constructed and objective realities that can be explained, in part, by existing sociological theories at the environmental and individual levels.

The Prevalence of Suicide in Modern Society

The CDC ranks suicide as a leading cause of death among Americans. In the U.S., suicide among people 10 years of age and older decreased slightly between 1991 and 2006, averaging between 14 and 15 deaths by suicide for every 100,000 people. A breakdown by age shows that the highest suicide rates per capita are for people over the age of 65, followed by those aged 25 to 64 years of age and 10 to 24 years of age respectively (CDC 2009).

While teen suicide rates are lower than those for the elderly, suicide is the third leading cause of death among teens (13–19), while it is the 11th leading cause of death among all other age groups (CDC 2007). In addition to this, many teenagers seriously consider suicide, i.e., experience suicide ideation, without attempting it. Alternatively, many others attempt, but do not complete suicide. For example, the CDC (2006) reports that in 2005, about one-fifth of all high school students reported seriously considering a recent suicide or attempted suicide. Of those who seriously considered suicide, about 50 percent attempted it. This translates to about 8 percent of all students attempting suicide.

The societal costs of teen suicide, self-harm, and suicide ideation extend beyond the loss of precious lives. Families and loved ones are troubled by extended periods of grief and mourning, and institutions that organize our society are disrupted. Consider that in 2004, there were an estimated 535,000 visits to U.S. hospital emergency departments for self-inflicted injuries (McCraig and Nawar 2006). In fact, Corso et al. (2007) estimated that the total lifetime costs of suicide and self-inflicted injuries for 2000 approximated $33 billion, including $1 billion for medical treatment and $32 billion for lost productivity. This exacts a considerable toll on health care facilities and the workplace, yet researchers estimate that a majority of people who engage in suicidal behavior never seek medical care (Diekstra 1982).

Variations by Race, Class, and Gender

One of the most compelling patterns about suicide is the difference between male and female rates. Looking at suicide in the general population, we find that males are much more likely to commit suicide than females. According to the CDC (2009), male suicide rates between 1991 and 2006 decreased but remained above 20 deaths per 100,000. Female rates were much lower, averaging about 5 deaths per 100,000 during the same time period. When we separate out teens from the general population, we find other interesting patterns. For example, females are more likely to consider suicide than male students in all racial or ethnic and grade level subgroups (CDC 2007), and girls in grades 9–11 were more likely to attempt suicide than males. In fact, the 2008 NSDUH found that teenage girls were much more likely than boys to report being depressed, which is a major individual-level predictor of suicide. However, male suicide rates far exceed those of females, perhaps because males of all ages favor a more efficient mechanism, e.g., firearms, in ending their lives than do females, e.g., suffocation and poisoning (CDC 2008). This helps explain the gender difference in deaths caused by suicide.

There are also patterns in teen suicide by race and ethnicity. According to the CDC (2008), suicide rates for persons between 10–24 years of age are highest for American Indians and Alaskan Natives. Between 2002 and 2006, their rates were 27.7 and 8.5 per 100,000 males and females respectively. White teens had the second highest suicide rate during the same time period: about 14 and 5 per 100,000 males and females respectively. Suicide among Black, Hispanic and Asian teens were similar to each other and lower than that for American Indians, Alaskan Natives and Whites.

Research on why teen suicide rates vary by race and ethnicity is relatively scarce. One of the few studies to address it, Colucci and Martin (2007), has noted difficulty in establishing clear patterns among groups, but concludes that the recent escalation of suicide among black male teens could also have something to do with Durkheim's ideas about integration, community, and individualism. The authors argue that the Black community has historically been characterized by **collectivism**, but that this has been broken down in the latter 20th century, leaving support for black males lacking. In the next section, I discuss explanations for suicide, paying particular attention to the continued relevance of Durkheim's structural functionalist approach in modern society.

Explanations of Suicide

It might seem as though explanations for a personal problem like suicide should be focused on individual or micro-level factors. Indeed, researchers from disciplines like psychology, psychiatry, and public health have published scores of studies on individual-level "risk" factors associated with teen self-injury, suicide, and suicide ideation. Risk factors are phenomena (e.g., traits, events, and experiences) believed to elevate the likelihood that something else (e.g., suicide) will happen. According to Donald et al. (2006) and the CDC (2008), things such as depression, childhood trauma, and low self-esteem constitute some of the best-documented risk factors for teen suicide. In fact suicide researchers (American Association of Suicidology 2010) have coined an acronym that represents the risk factors commonly found to explain why individuals are suicidal: IS PATH WARM:

> Ideation, Substance Abuse
> Purposelessness, Anxiety, Trapped, Hopelessness
> Withdrawal, Anger, Recklessness, Mood Changes

While such risk factors can help identify suicidal youth (i.e., a step toward combating the problem—see Chapter V for more), they do not constitute a theory of suicide and often provide only a short-term fix. A theory of suicide could help explain the big picture and chart an effective course of action over the long term. Enter sociology and the work of Emile Durkheim.

In a classic book, Durkheim (1951) argued that suicide was the result of societies with extreme integration patterns, i.e., people were either too tightly committed to each other (communal) or too independent from one another (individualistic). In the first case, **altruistic suicide** resulted because individuals failed to meet a community standard or gave their lives to uphold one. In the second case, **egoistic suicide** resulted because the independent, free individual had no ties to others and suffered alienation as a result. Durkheim maintained that egoistic suicide would characterize nations like the U.S., with advanced capitalist economies and political and cultural prioritization of individual freedom. It would seem the CDC agrees with Durkheim about egoistic suicide, since they recently advocated promoting connectedness among persons, families, and communities to combat it. They claimed "Connectedness is a common thread that weaves together many of the influences of suicidal behavior and has direct relevance for prevention" (CDC 2008: 3).

A recent development on the immensely popular social networking site Facebook calls this into question and provides an example of just how difficult it is to balance the integration styles to prevent things like suicide. Facebook has enabled people worldwide to celebrate their individuality, reconnect with old friends and family, and expand their interaction and bonds with friendship and other (e.g., political, cultural, leisure, etc.) communities. On the surface, it would appear that Facebook embodies a perfect balance between the integration styles (i.e., communal and individualistic—see Chapter I) that Durkheim and other structural functionalists claimed were necessary for a stable society. Recently, however, Facebook has been linked to a variety of youth problems, including "virtual" as well as actual suicide. Let's consider **virtual suicide** on Facebook.

According to an article posted by Emma Justice at TimesOnline.com (2007), Stephanie Painter—a 27-year-old Londoner—died a swift and painless virtual death at 9.10pm on February 11 with a simple click of her mouse. She claimed that "Facebook was damaging my relationship with my boyfriend to such an extent that if I hadn't done it we wouldn't be together now." Like the more than 400 million users worldwide, Painter was an enthusiastic Facebooker who used the site to reconnect with old and new friends. Soon, however, she found that this seemingly innocent way of interacting with others opened up, instead, a dangerous can of worms. After constant fights with her boyfriend, Painter completed virtual suicide by using the Facebook Mass Suicide Club application to delete her account before it "consumed her." Within seconds, Painter's virtual death was complete.

Even though Facebook's technical brilliance and global dominance have convinced many that it can help them balance their individuality with community-like connections to other people and various socio-political causes, it too suffers from the Durkheimian quagmire of integration in modern society, where the trend toward one extreme or the other can lead to suicide, i.e., virtual suicide in this case. Matt Holm, a 24-year-old Facebook user from London, sums it up, "When I was introduced to friends of friends, they'd recognize me from my profile on Facebook. I no longer had any anonymity and that was disconcerting" (Justice 2007).

Connections to Sexuality and Substance Abuse

By now, it should be clear that the three types of youth problems discussed in this book are interconnected. Still, we need to think more about this, including not only *that* they are connected but *how* they are. There are a few ways to do this. One is to identify focal points or over-arching issues where each of the three problems of sexuality, substance use, and suicide converge. A second approach would be to ascertain a causal explanation or model with independent and dependent variables, like we discussed in Chapter I. One such model might address if being abused as a child leads to substance use and suicide later on. Both of these approaches are common in sociological research, so let's consider each in turn.

From the pages above, we can glean at least two focal points to connect the three youth problems discussed in this book. The first is the family. We now know that parental substance abuse increases the risk of child abuse. Children abused by their parents or other adults are more likely to get involved in sexual behaviors earlier than others and many of these activities lead to sex–related problems, such as teen pregnancy, STDs and HIV, and exposure to abusive intimate relationships. Parental substance use also increases the risks of a child's own substance use, via the family transmission thesis. Both sexual victimization and substance abuse have been linked repeatedly to teen suicide. A simple look at the IS PATH WARM acronym provides evidence of this. Not convinced? Then the recent blog post below by 14-year-old Hannah at www.suicideproject.org might convince you. It not only supports the risk factors listed in the IS PATH WARM acronym, it hints at family abuse, neglect, and substance use that make Hannah think about ending her life (i.e., suicide ideation):

> My name is Hannah. I'm a severe self-harmer. I cut, burn, hit, anything to feel pain. I've been hospitalized 3 times because of it. I've also been hospitalized for Bulimia Nevosa, which I've been suffering from for 2 years. I have Bipolar–depression, GAD (generalized anxiety disorder), agrophobia, and PTSD. I've been having a hard time lately. Schools out, which means nothing can distract me from my life. My addictions. My 'drugs'. It seems like everything is spinning out of control. Emotions turning left and right and left again. I'm keeping secret after secret after secret. I'm lying about everything. My emotions. My problems. Myself. Everything. I feel like I'm throwing my life down the toilet, literally. But the issue is, I don't care anymore. Just lie down and sleep and never wake up. I've just given up. On everything. Nothings enough anymore. I loose 5 pounds a week, purging and binging and purging and sleeping and crying and passing out and lying and keeping the secrets. I've got lots of them. I'm not going to tell you my past, but let's just say it was filled with rape, abuse, drugs, alcohol, death, and pain. Lots and lots of pain and I'm 14 years old.
>
> (Comment posted in June 2010 on Rants blog at www.suicideproject.com)

The family is not, however, the only place to understand the link between these three youth problems. Adolescent identity development is another. As discussed earlier, adolescent identity development is a fragile, yet critical process for teens to negotiate.

Numerous people and institutions, in addition to the family, play a role in it. Friends, teachers, coaches, and religious and community leaders are among the most important influences on youth identity. Institutions like schools, churches, and the media exert still more pressure. Since the period of adolescent identity development is dominated by sexuality (i.e., discovering who one is physically and emotionally attracted to and cares to interact with) and gender (e.g., masculinity and femininity) concerns, it is necessary to understand the social expectations that people and institutions have about those things for youth in our society.

In the U.S., sexuality and gender identity adhere to what sociologists call **heteronormative** standards (Butler 1990). This includes fashioning one's identity according to the traits of traditional **masculinity** and **femininity** and orienting one's behaviors to heterosexual relationships. Obviously, heteronormative standards create problems for gay, lesbian, and bisexual youth. As we have already discussed, this leads some to substance use or self-harm and injury. However, heternormative standards also create tension for heterosexuals as they disallow freedom of expression and behavior (Butler 1990) and exert pressure to conform to extreme versions of masculinity and femininity. For example, two graduates students and I (Anderson et al. 2009b) recently found that hyper-masculine identity needs were associated with physical and sexual assault among young adults at both hip hop and electronic dance music nightclub events. Sexual desires and relationships motivated masculine identity contests and, when coupled with alcohol, increased the risk of physical and sexual assault. From this, we learn that adolescent identity development is influenced by heteronormative standards and expectations and that these pressures lead to substance use and abuse and other problematic behaviors.

A second approach in understanding the connections between social problems lies in ascertaining causality through models with independent and dependent variables. In other words, do sexuality problems cause substance use and suicide? Social scientists ask questions about the root of social problems because they are interested in identifying causes so that effective solutions can be advocated and implemented (Bachman and Schutt 2007). However, this is often a difficult undertaking because the criteria of causality are much more difficult to meet than simply identifying a focal point where things converge.

Causality begins with articulating **hypotheses** from theories, such as structural functionalism and others mentioned above. Hypotheses are specific statements of a relationship between two or more theoretical constructs or variables. Hypotheses have independent and dependent variables, which suppose that something (independent variable) has an effect on something else (dependent variable). In our case, does being sexually abused as a child act as an independent variable to cause teen substance use and suicide (two dependent variables)? Alternatively, does child abuse cause substance use and then does substance use, in turn, lead to suicide? There are numerous possibilities, thus making causal explanations of social problems quite difficult to establish.

Researchers maintain that at least three criteria must be met to establish causality. First, all of the variables must show an empirical correlation with each other. For example, sexual abuse, drug use, and suicide must be scientifically related. Second, there must be a proper time order established between independent and dependent variables. In other words, to claim that child abuse causes substance use, one must show that the child abuse victimization happened before the victim started using substances. This criterion may be easier to establish since sexual victimization happens in childhood and teen substance use happens later on. However, it becomes harder to meet this standard with substance use and suicide. Finally, the relationship between the independent and dependent variables cannot be spurious or due to some outside force or factor that artificially implies a real connection.

We can return to the case of Megan Meier to consider spuriousness and the other criteria of cause. If cyber-bullying is a cause of Megan's suicide, then the cyber-bullying would have had to occur before she took her life. It did, so the temporal ordering criterion of cause, i.e., that the independent variable (cyber-bullying) precedes the dependent variable (Megan's suicide), has been met. Let us then assume, absent any proof, that there is a correlation between cyber-bullying and Megan's suicide and those of others, keeping in mind that social scientists would need to verify this empirically. This assumption would satisfy the second criterion of cause: correlation between independent and dependent variables. It is the spuriousness criterion of cause that may pose the biggest challenge to the simple explanation that cyber-bullying caused Megan's death. How can we be certain that some other factor, e.g., Megan's low self-esteem or prescription medications, are not artificially producing a relationship between cyber-bullying and her death? There are numerous ways social scientists address this third criterion of cause, including building and testing explanatory models with many independent variables. The details of these procedures are, however, beyond the scope of this book.

Conclusions

Suicide is something that stirs our emotions and raises our attention. It does not matter that it is less prevalent than some other problem behaviors (e.g., drug dependence, property crime, physical assault). The taking of one's own life is considered a tragedy in our society and many others. And even though rates of suicide are higher for the elderly and adults, teen suicide is considered especially problematic due to the innocence of childhood and the social expectations we have of young people in our society. This helps explain why any potentially new causes (e.g., cyber-bullying via websites) and changes in the methods of suicide (e.g., increases in overdoses from certain prescribed drugs) trouble us.

While we know that youth sexuality, substance use, and suicide are interrelated social problems, it is certainly more perplexing to understand how. In this book, I have reviewed many studies that offer some scientific evidence of causal relationships between sexuality, substance use, and suicide. In fact, the ordering of this book's chapters is no accident, as research supports that sexuality problems more often lead to substance use and suicide than any other combination of the three. Still, as sociologists we know that social problems have numerous causes, that those causes might differ depending on the group we study or the intersection of identities of the people we investigate, and that such explanations might shift over time. The challenges we face in ascertaining the difference between claims about the causes of social problems, like suicide, and scientifically based facts are considerable. And it is a fundamental sociological goal to utilize the research process to distinguish ordinary and sensational claims about youth social problems from observable scientific facts.

DISCUSSION QUESTIONS

1. Considering the intersectionality of our identities, what do you think are the cultural, social, and economic factors that explain differences in suicide rates between males and females and the diverse race and ethnic groups that live in the U.S.?

2. Discuss the pros and cons of using quantitative surveys like the National Survey on Drug Use and Health and Youth Risk Behavior Survey to study suicide among youth. What else could we learn about the topic if we used in-depth interviews or some other qualitative methodology?

V: Sociological Solutions
to Youth Problems

~~~~~~

Introduction

As we come to the end of this book, I'd like to discuss how sociologists try to remedy social problems, including those discussed in this book. While the information presented in the previous chapters can be depressing, the good news is that there are many solutions to the problems youth and young adults face and millions of people, including **social problems workers**, willing to help. In addition, as our society has advanced, we have become much better at determining which programs work best and are most efficient. As indicated in previous chapters, rates of teen pregnancy, HIV, substance use and dependence, and suicide have dropped or have leveled off between the late 20th century and the early 21st century. Effective policies and programs are partially responsible for this success. Still, history shows these rates fluctuate with social and economic trends, necessitating our constant attention. Moreover, there are signs of new youth problems on our horizon, including those related to new technologies (e.g., cyber-bullying on the internet and social networking sites) and growing industries (e.g., non-medical use of prescription drugs from pharmaceutical companies and the increased **medicalization** of our society—Conrad 2007). Thus, **social problems work** with youth, young adults, and others will constantly evolve and require our consideration.

Before discussing some of the types of solutions, an important point should be made about the difficulties in addressing youth social problems. Things like hooking up, premarital sex, or teen marijuana use are not considered problematic by all people. Recall this is what the social construction approach teaches us. Social problems are both subjective and objective. And even when a behavior is considered troublesome, it may not be defined in the same fashion by those who care about it. For example, some consider teen drug use a criminal matter while others view it as a public health problem. The point is that without agreement about whether a problem really exists or what its nature is, effective solutions are difficult to come by. In the remainder of this chapter, then, I discuss concrete solutions to what people believe to be real youth problems. In doing so, I acknowledge that despite disagreement in how behaviors are defined, there remain consequences that people want to see eliminated.

Types of Solutions

Our society has many different kinds of solutions to combat the types of problem discussed in this book. They can be categorized in numerous ways and they feature a wide range of institutions and actors. While most target the very people who engage in problematic behaviors, e.g., the teens who abuse drugs or attempt suicide, there are also solutions for those impacted by their actions, like parents and other family members. In this chapter, I discuss solutions for the teens and young adults in trouble since they are the book's primary focus.

Solutions and interventions come in four main varieties: prevention, punishment, treatment, and rehabilitation or re-entry. These are the most common responses to the problems and populations discussed in this book. **Prevention programs** try to make sure problematic behavior never occurs in the first place or is not allowed to materialize into anything too serious. **Punishment policies** seek to deter people from engaging in problem behaviors by threatening sanctions and penalties usually in a formal fashion. **Treatment programs** tend to be health-oriented as they address biomedical, physical, and mental causes, symptoms and complications of the problem behavior. Finally, **rehabilitation and re-entry programs** aim to change individuals' behavior to be more law-abiding and conventional so that they desist from deviance and become upstanding members of society.

The People and Resources Behind Youth Programs

Another way to classify solutions is by who administers and funds them. Many federal, state, and local government agencies exist to address sexuality, substance use, and suicide among teens and young adults. At the federal level, the more prominent ones are the Centers for Disease Control (CDC), the National Institute on Drug Abuse (NIDA), the Substance Abuse and Mental Health Services Administration (SAMHSA), and the Administration for Children and Families (ACF). Federal agencies like these receive monies from the President in his annual budget, which must be approved by Congress. Federal agencies then turn around and pass out the money they receive to the states for direct services. So, it is mostly at the state and local levels where we find programs that deliver actual services to individuals and groups troubled by sexual, substance use, and suicide problems. Monies are also passed out to researchers, including sociologists, to produce knowledge on how to combat the problems (see more below). Thus, continued research is part of the solution to social problems. I discuss this more below.

Social problems are not only addressed and funded by governments. In fact, there are more private agencies that do so and they spend more money collectively than do all government agencies combined (Kendall 2010). It's beyond the scope of this book to describe all of the private efforts that go into solving problems associated with youth sexuality, substance use and suicide. For sure, they include churches and religious institutions (e.g., the YMCA), non-governmental organizations (e.g., United Way), corporations (many have philanthropic foundations to promote social good, e.g., Johnson and Johnson has the Robert Wood Johnson Foundation to combat substance abuse), and self-help (e.g., Alcoholics Anonymous) and support groups of all varieties.

Self-help and other community-based support groups are especially important since they cost very little and are quite effective. For example, there are hundreds, if not thousands, of online chat rooms and communities offering support for people considering suicide, recovering from failed attempts at it, or who have been impacted someone's suicide (see www.suicideproject.org and www.survivorsofsuicide.com). They are even more for sexuality-based issues, such as survivors of incest and sexual abuse, sexual assault and rape, GLBT teens, etc. It seems as though such groups are even more abundant for substance use and abuse issues and populations.

Prevention as Key to Combating Youth Social Problems

To reiterate an earlier point, prevention programs are the primary way our society, and its social problems institutions and stakeholders, address youth issues. The philosophy behind prevention programs is to either disallow the issue or behavior from occurring in the first place or to prevent it from materializing into a full-scale problem with lots of consequences. Prevention programs are preferred because it is cheaper to nip something in the bud early on rather than trying to fix a problem after it has exploded. Also, letting issues become full-scale social problems threatens irreversible consequences, which may be resilient to other types of interventions.

It is necessary to make a few important points about prevention programs' work in solving the youth problems related to sexuality, substance use, and suicide. First, prevention programs are typically favored in solving or addressing youth problems for reasons consistent with labeling theory and symbolic interactionism. Since prevention programs seek to block problems from either happening in the first place or inhibit them from becoming serious matters, they are especially suited to young people so that we can prevent them, i.e., the future of society, from becoming enmeshed in deviant careers or problematic behavioral lifestyles throughout their lives. This viewpoint recognizes that the stigmatizing effects of punishment (arrest, school suspension) can act to cement the young into deviant career patterns via formal social control and the self-fulfilling prophecy. Second, prevention strategies in the area of sexuality, substance use, and suicide are often defined as public health matters, rather than criminal ones. This is evident from looking at the federal agencies, e.g., CDC, NIDA and other institutes of the Offices of Health and Human Services that address these problems. While underage drinking and taking one's life are illegal acts, prevention approaches view them as physical and mental health issues in need of medical understanding and responses. The goal becomes to educate youth and their families about the various consequences that come from premarital risky sex, binge drinking, and self-injury and to treat the health complications from such activities.

Preventing youth problems happens at numerous levels and through various forms. **Primary prevention** takes aim at the population at large, irrespective of the relative risk of problems. These are the programs that seek to prevent behavior before it ever happens (Kendall 2010). Examples include public service announcements on TV, at the movies, or on the Internet warning about the potential health complications. We can easily find examples of such announcements or advertisements in the area of youth drug and alcohol use. The federal government's Office of National Drug Control Policy runs a separate webpage dedicated to preventing youth substance abuse via TV and other media announcements called the National Youth Anti-Drug Media Campaign (http://www.whitehousedrugpolicy.gov/mediacampaign/index.html). There are numerous TV, radio, print, and web-based media campaigns designed to prevent youth substance use by educating students about the consequences of drugs and alcohol and helping them develop skills to resist using them. Most school-based sex, drug, and alcohol programs are also considered primary prevention efforts.

Secondary prevention programs hone in on youth considered at high risk of engaging in the problematic behaviors. This would include abused, homeless, and delinquent youth. Direct efforts are tailored to these at-risk kids and young adults, making secondary prevention goals quite different to the more general ones associated with primary prevention (Kendall 2010). An example of a secondary prevention program would be posting warning posters about drunk driving and fetal alcohol syndrome in nightclubs frequented by the young men and women profiled in Chapter III.

Tertiary prevention programs are for individuals who have already experienced a sex, drug, alcohol, or self-injury problem. Examples of them would be providing condoms to teens engaged in premarital sex to reduce pregnancy and contracting STDs or HIV. Tertiary prevention programs also encourage those affected to seek treatment for reducing the health-related complications of their conditions or from certain behaviors. This includes making sure that youth who get services to stop problems behaviors remain that way after the program ends. So in many ways, they are like treatment programs (Kendall 2010). This is why many substance abuse programs incorporate self-help groups into their regimens. Programs like Alcoholics Anonymous, Narcotics Anonymous, and Cocaine Anonymous help alcoholics and addicts stay drug and alcohol free on a daily basis, treating the conditions as permanently in remission.

Within primary, secondary, and tertiary programs, a variety of prevention models are also employed. These models are based on implicit or explicit theories about why people use and abuse alcohol, tobacco and other drugs. Thus, in the paragraphs below, I discuss the kinds of prevention efforts structural functionalism, conflict theory, and symbolic interactionism advocate. Before doing so, it is useful to define some of these prevention models.

One of the oldest and most prevalent types of prevention programs is the **informa-tion model**. This model teaches youth about the dangers and consequences associ-ated with certain behaviors and surmises that such knowledge will cause them to avoid such behavior. The **social norms model** attempts to change problematic beliefs and values that may have been passed onto youth from their parents or other signifi-cant people in their lives. The argument goes, for example, that marijuana use can be reduced by changing beliefs about the social acceptability of it. **Life skills models** attempt to get people to turn their newfound knowledge on the dangers of certain behaviors into concrete, positive action. The focus is on helping youth acquire new life skills in the areas of problem-solving, self-esteem, alternatives to stress, resisting peer pressure, and improved communication. **Proscriptive prevention programs** are like punishment, in that they increase the costs and penalties associated with things like premarital sex, substance use, and suicide attempts. Chapter I's discussion of raising the drinking age is an example of a proscriptive prevention program. Also, increasing penalties for tobacco sales to minors is another. Finally, the **environmental model** of prevention is based on reducing the availability of opportunities for problem behavior. These programs focus on community characteristics and the interplay of laws, policies, commercial establishments, and social institutions therein.

Sociologists' Role in Combating Social Problems

In general, sociologists believe that the best solutions to social problems are those that emanate from the theory and research that provides evidence on the causes of those problems. In this book, I discussed three major sociological paradigms (i.e., structural functionalism, conflict theory, and symbolic interactionism) used to explain youth sexuality, substance use, and suicide. Thus, there are different kinds of solutions to each of the problems since these three approaches favor individual or environmental and structural factors to explain the causes of youth problems. To recall, micro theo-ries, like labeling theory and symbolic interactionism, focus on micro-level or people-centered solutions, while structural and environmental theories call for macro-level and institutional changes in society.

Environmental Prevention Programs and Structural Functionalism

Recall the work of Durkheim, Merton, and Agnew discussed in Chapters I, III and IV. It called attention to imbalances between societal goals for material success and a decent standard of living and the absence of legitimate opportunities to obtain them. At a basic level, then, structural functionalists maintain that policies or programs that either increase people's access to legitimate opportunities for goal attainment, or reduce their aspirations for them, will likely reduce social problems and their deleteri-ous effects. This problem-solving approach falls in line with environmental prevention programs. For example, Merton's work helped inspire the Juvenile Delinquency and Control Act of 1961 (Anderson n.d.), which targeted many types of youth substance use and related matters. This Act provided employment and training, along with community organization and improved social services, to disadvantaged youths and their families. The program was later expanded to become the foundation for Johnson's War on Poverty. Also, billions of dollars were spent on programs in the 1960s, such as the Peace Corps, Jobs Corps, Comprehensive Employee Training Act (CETA), and Project Head Start. Shortly after their creation, however, Nixon discontinued most of them, arguing that they had failed to achieve their goals (Anderson n.d.).

Before these efforts, sociologists advocated other environmental prevention programs featuring neighborhood initiatives to combat an array of youth problems. Theorizing that youth deviance resulted from social disorganization, Shaw and McKay (1969) advocated neighborhood empowerment programs to assist people in fighting community and individual problems. The goal of such programs is to use government support to sponsor socially positive activities that help individuals bond with each other to strengthen their communities against crime, drugs, and deviance. If you'll recall, this is what Durkheim had in mind when discussing the importance of anomie, integration, and solidarity. Such programs might include summer camps and sports leagues, as well as housing supports to reverse neighborhood deterioration. For example, during the Clinton administration, Attorney General Janet Reno proposed funding midnight basketball programs to achieve this purpose. During the late 1980s and early 1990s Senator Jack Kemp advocated community empowerment zones that would replace abandoned housing with new units to be purchased by lower income families. Policy makers argued that individual investment and improved housing conditions would bolster people's stakes in and ties to their communities while increasing property values. Community integration, increased solidarity, and reductions in deviance would result. While efforts like these decreased during the Bush presidency, they still are considered viable in combating youth and other social problems by more recent scholars (Sampson and Raudenbusch 1999; Sampson, Raudenbush, and Felton 1997).

Conflict Theory Solutions

Conflict theorists are most likely to call for macro-level social change that targets eliminating or reducing various forms on inequality in society. Social change focuses on the long term by empowering individuals with capital and changing institutions and the laws, cultural ideals, and policies that structure society. This is how social reproduction scholars have addressed a variety of youth delinquency (e.g., drugs and crime) problems (Bourgois 1996; MacLeod 1987).

The conflict approach also draws on environmental prevention policies by reducing inequality through programs that empower people. Scholars from this perspective have also proposed scaling back punishment and punitive policies in general so as to quell the negative effects they have on offenders. This latter recommendation is shared by interactionists (see below); however, conflict theorists tend to advocate solutions for groups, while interactionists more often do so for individuals.

Wrap-around models are a fairly new approach to solving social problems, especially those that impact youth and their families. They take a long-term and broad approach to issues and feature coordinating a range of services—like family therapy, vocational training, parenting classes, substance abuse counseling, etc.—that are 'wrapped around' families in a helpful and empathetic fashion (Morrison-Velasco 2000). Thus, they seek to empower people with various resources so that they can better function in modern society. This makes them consistent with conflict theory premises.

Life Skills, Social Norms, and Symbolic Interactionism

Finally, scholars advocating solutions from labeling theory and other symbolic interactionist approaches focus on the relationship between social institutions and actors and the very individuals engaged in the problem behavior. Interactionists believe that formal social controls and heavy punishments for youth deviance worsen the problem by creating stigma and self-fulfilling prophecies. Instead, they advocate "softer" solutions that include, for example, decriminalization of drugs like marijuana or using restorative justice or re-integrative shaming programs (Braithwaite 1989) to enable youth to make amends to people they've harmed. These efforts reduce the lasting implications of stigma. For labeling theorists, reducing the severity of the formal social reaction to deviance would reduce the lasting impact of stigma on the so-called deviant or offender.

The closely related social control theory takes a different approach to reconciling the link between problem youth and social institutions. It focuses on how young people are socialized, making it consistent with the social norms model of prevention. Such efforts must, advocates contend, promote the development of a strong moral bond to society and increased self-control. Resources and programs offering parent training and functional family therapies facilitate this goal. If children reside in extremely problematic families, group homes and surrogate families might be a necessary option. Finally, other important socialization agencies, like the schools, can make available counseling and problem-solving and social skills training with 'at risk' children.

Social learning theories focus, instead, on positive and negative reinforcements on behavior, especially among adolescents. Thus, solutions for problems like teen substance abuse would likely be to increase the efficiency and effectiveness of social controls on deviant behavior (e.g., penalties and sanctions) and increased rewards for non-deviant or conforming behaviors, making this micro-level theory more consistent with punitive solutions and unlike other interactionist theories. Such punitive responses have yielded little progress in stemming drug use, abuse, and related social and criminal consequences. Perhaps, then, a wiser approach would be to increase reinforcement of positive behaviors. Rewarding kids for conventional activities, saying no to drugs, and helping them to develop anti-drug skills are commonly conveyed in drug use prevention programs like D.A.R.E. and youth-targeted media campaigns. These strategies follow the life skills prevention model. However, engaging in such activities and developing such anti-drug skills likely requires resources: recreational, education, and economic opportunities and new resource allocations for prevention programs. Thus, combining the life skills and environmental strategies approaches may be an especially valuable weapon to combat youth social problems.

Intersectionality: One Size Does Not Solve All

While there are many promising solutions available to combat youth social problems related to sexuality, substance use, and suicide, and an army of people active and willing to help, we must bear in mind a point made back in Chapter I: social problems are experienced differently for youth depending on their backgrounds. Thus, intersectionality teaches that solutions cannot come in 'one size' for all people. They should be tailored by group in order to be most effective. This is a point the big three theories of sociology overlooked for a long time, but have gotten on board within the latter part of the 20th century. For example, research has found that increasing ethnic identity pride helps decrease drug use among African-American youth, but doesn't seem to help white teens (Marsiglia, Kulis, and Hecht 2001). On the contrary, the acculturation of minority groups, i.e., pressure to abandon traditional cultural traits and beliefs for those of mainstream America, are associated with increased rates of drug and alcohol abuse (Amaro et al. 1990). These studies indicate the importance, relevance, and complicated nature of interactionist and labeling theory in understanding teen substance use issues in a diverse society.

In my own research on drug abusers (Anderson 1998a–d), I have found that the processes of becoming addicted to drugs and alcohol were intimately tied to the various identity needs and experiences unique to males and females from different racial groups. For example, both black males and females were more likely than their white counterparts to experience personal alienation at school and later tie such experiences to substance abuse. I also found important race-related differences in educational and economic opportunities, which were also linked to substance use. Addressing these differences would likely draw on the life skills and environmental prevention models, but in unique ways for teens from different backgrounds. This underscores the importance of intersectionality in dealing with youth substance use and related problems.

The federal government currently hosts an innovative website for teens (www. abovetheinfluence.com) that recognizes the role of the diverse identity needs among racially and ethnically mixed males and females in resisting and recovering from sex, drug, alcohol, and depression-related problems. Teens and young adults are encouraged to post their stories via text, photos, artwork, and videos to share their stories with others in a sort of information and social norms approach to help others like them. This unique and cutting-edge solution helps teens take responsibility for helping themselves and others, with the support of public and private institutions and actors. Programs like abovetheinfluence thus not only perfectly embody the sociological approach to youth social problems, they are among the most promising in helping young people survive the daily threats of sexual abuse, drug and alcohol abuse, and depression and death.

References

Abma, J. C., G. M. Martinez, W. D. Mosher, and B. S. Dawson. 2004. "Teenagers in the United States: Sexual Activity, Contraception Use, and Childbearing, 2002". National Center for Health Statistics. *Vital Health Stat, 23*(24): 1–87.

Administration on Children and Families. 2008. *Child Maltreatment 2008.* Rockville, MD: Department of Health and Human Services.

Agnew, Robert. 2006. *Pressured into Crime: an Overview of General Strain Theory.* Los Angeles: Roxbury.

Allan, Kenneth. 2007. *The Social Lens: An Invitation to Social and Sociological Theory.* Thousand Oaks, CA: Sage Publications.

Amaro, H., R. Whitaker, G. Coffman, and T. Heeren. 1990. "Acculturation and Marijuana and Cocaine Use: Findings from HHANES 1982–84," *American Journal of Public Health, 80*(suppl): 54–60.

American Association of Suicidology. 2010. *Lesbian, Gay, Bisexual and Transgendered Resource Sheet.* Washington, DC. Retrieved June 15, 2010 (http://www.suicidology.org).

Anderson, Tammy L. 1993. "Types of Identity Transformation in Drug Using and Recovery Careers." *Sociological Focus, 26*: 133–45.

———. 1994. 'Drug Abuse and Identity: Linking Micro and Macro Factors." *Sociological Quarterly, 35*(1): 159–74.

———. 1998a. "A Cultural-Identity Theory of Drug Abuse." *The Sociology of Crime, Law, and Deviance, 1*: 233–62.

———. 1998b. "Drug Identity Change Processes, Race, and Gender: Part 1. Explanations of Drug Misuse and a New Identity-Based Model." *Substance Use and Misuse, 33*(11): 2263–79.

———. 1998c. "Drug Identity Change Processes, Race, and Gender: Part 2. Micro-Level Motivational Concepts." *Substance Use and Misuse, 33*(12): 2469–83.

———. 1998d. "Drug Identity Change Processes, Race, and Gender: Part 3. Macro-Level Opportunity Concepts." *Substance Use and Misuse, 33*(14): 2721–35.

———. 2005. "Dimensions of Women's Power in the Illicit Drug Economy," *Theoretical Criminology, 9*(4): 271–400.

———. n.d. "Sociological Theories of Drug Abuse," in progress for Harrison, L., Anderson, T., Martin, S., and Robbins, C. *Drug and Alcohol Use in Social Context.* Belmont, CA: Wadsworth Publishing.

Anderson, Tammy L., Philip R. Kavanaugh, Ronet Bachman, and Lana D. Harrison. 2007. *Exploring the Drugs-Crime Connection within the Electronic Dance and Hip-Hop Nightclub Scenes, Final Report.* Washington, DC: U.S. Department of Justice.

Anderson, Tammy L., Philip R. Kavanaugh, Kevin Daly, and Laura Rapp. 2009a. "Clubbing Masculinities and Crime: A Qualitative Study of Philadelphia Nightclub Scenes." *Feminist Criminology, 4*(4): 302–32.

Anderson, Tammy L., Philip R. Kavanaugh, Laura Rapp, and Kevin Daly. 2009b. "Variations in Clubbers' Substance Abuse Careers by Individual- and Scene-Level Factors." *Adicciones, 21*(4): 302–32.

Associated Press. 2010 (June 17). "Arizona Couple Arrested after Abuse Baby Dies." Retrieved June 17, 2010 (http://www.google.com/hostednews/ap/article/ALeqM5gnrStVptysX0V-1PLCloinnUV2swD9GCLDDG0).

Bachman, Ronet, and Linda Saltzman. 1995. *Violence Against Women: Estimates from the Redesigned Survey.* Washington, DC: Bureau of Justice Statistics, U.S. Department of Justice.

Bachman, Ronet, and Russell K. Schutt. 2007. *The Practice of Research in Criminology and Criminal Justice.* Los Angeles: Sage Publications.

Bailey, Beth L. 1988. *From Front Porch to Back Seat: Courtship in Twentieth-Century America.* Baltimore: The Johns Hopkins University Press.

Bassoff, E. S., and G. V. Glass. 1982. "The Relationship Between Sex Roles and Mental Health: A Meta-Analysis of Twenty-Six Studies." *Counseling Psychologist, 10*: 105–12 10.1177/0011000082104019.

Becker, Howard S. 1963. *Outsiders: Studies in the Sociology of Deviance.* New York, NY: The Free Press.

Behman, R. E., R. M. Kliegman, and A. M. Arvin (eds.). 1996. *Nelson Textbook of Pediatrics.* 15th ed. Philadelphia, PA: W. B. Saunders Company.

Bennett, Andy. 2001. *Cultures of Popular Music.* Buckingham, UK: Open University Press.

Berkey-Gerard, Mark. 2001. "Neighbors and Nightclubs." *Gotham Gazette,* May 5.

Black, Maureen, Sarah E. Oberlander, Terri Lewis, Elizabeth D. Knight, Adam J. Zolotor, Alan J. Litrownik, Richard Thompson, Howard Dubowitz, and Diana E. English. 2009. "Sexual Intercourse Among Adolescents Maltreated Before Age 12: A Prospective Investigation," *Pediatrics, 124*(3), September: 941–49.

Blumer, Herbert. 1969. *Symbolic Interactionism: Perspective and Method.* Berkeley: University of California Press.

Bogle, Kathleen. 2008. *Hooking Up: Sex, Dating, and Relationships on Campus.* New York: New York University Press.

Bogle, Kathleen. 2009. "The Shift from Dating to Hooking Up in College: What Scholars have Missed." *Sociology Compass, 1*(2): 775–88.

Bourdieu, Pierre. 1977. "Cultural Reproduction and Social Reproduction." In J. Karabel and A. H. Halsey (eds.), *Power and Ideology in Education.* New York: Oxford University Press, pp. 487–511.

Bourdieu, Pierre, and Jean-Claude Passeron. (eds.) 1990. *Reproduction in Education, Society and Culture,* 2nd ed. London: Sage Publications.

Bourgois, Phillippe. 1996. *In Search of Respect*. New York: Cambridge University Press.

Braithwaite, John. 1989. *Crime, Shame and Reintegration*. Cambridge: Cambridge University Press.

Bronfenbrenner, U. 1989. "Ecological Systems Theory." *Annals of Child Development*, 16, 187–249.

Brotherton, David. 2004. *The Almighty Latin King and Queen Nation: Street Politics and the Transformation of a New York City Gang*. New York: Columbia University Press.

Buddie, Amy M., and Kathleen A. Parks. 2003. "The Role of the Bar Context and Social Behaviors on Women's Risk for Aggression." *Journal of Interpersonal Violence* 18: 1378–93.

Butler, J. 1990. *Gender Trouble: Feminism and the Subversion of Identity*. New York: Routledge.

Catalano, S. M. 2005. *Criminal Victimization, 2004*. Washington, DC: Bureau of Justice Statistics, U.S. Department of Justice.

CDC (Centers for Disease Control and Prevention). 2000. "Sexually Transmitted Diseases." In *Healthy People 2010: Volume II: Objectives for Improving Health (Part B, Focus Area 25)*. 2nd edition. Retrieved May 10, 2010. (http://www.cdc.gov/ncipc/dvp/Suicide/youthsuicide.htm).

———. 2006. "Youth Risk Behavior Surveillance: United States, 2005." *MMWR, 55*(SS–5): 1–108. June 9.

———. 2008. *Promoting Individual, Family, and Community Connectedness to Prevent Suicidal Behavior*. Atlanta, GA: Centers for Disease Control and Prevention. National Center for Injury Prevention and Control.

———. 2009. "National Suicide Statistics at a Glance." Retrieved May 10, 2010 (http://www.cdc.gov/violenceprevention/suicide/statistics/trends01.html).

———. 2010. "Healthy Youth: Sexual Risk Behaviors." Atlanta, GA: CDC. Retrieved May 10, 2010 (http://www.cdc.gov/HealthyYouth/sexualbehaviors/index.htm).

CDC, National Center for Injury Prevention and Control. 2007. *Youth Suicide* (cited August 8, 2008). (http://www.cdc.gov/ncipc/dvp/Suicide/youthsuicide.htm).

Center for Alcohol Marketing and Youth. 2008. *Youth Exposure to Alcohol Advertising on Television, 2001–2007*. Washington, D.C.: Georgetown University.

Chatterton, Paul, and Robert Hollands. 2002. "Theorising Urban Playscapes: Producing, Regulating And Consuming Youthful Nightlife City Spaces." *Urban Studies, 39*: 95–116.

Child Welfare website (n.d.). Retrieved June 11, 2010 (http://www.childwelfare.gov/can/factors/parentcaregiver/substance.cfm).

Collins, Patricia Hill. 2007. "Pushing The Boundaries or Business as Usual: Race, Class, and Gender Studies and Sociological Inquiry." In C. Calhoun (ed.), *Sociology in America: A History*. Chicago: University of Chicago Press, pp. 527–604.

Colucci, Erminia, and Graham Martin. 2007. "Ethnocultural Aspects of Suicide in Young People: A Systematic Literature Review. Part 1: Rates and Methods of Suicide." *Suicide and Life-Threatening Behavior, 37*(2): 197–221.

Conrad, P. 2007. *The Medicalization of Society: On the Transformation of Human Conditions into Treatable Disorders*. Baltimore: John's Hopkins University Press.

Cooley, Charles. 1922. *Social Process*. New York: Scribners.

———. 1998. *On Self and Social Organization*. Chicago: University of Chicago Press.

Corso, P. S., J. A. Mercy, T. R. Simon, E. A. Finkelstein, and T. R. Miller. 2007. "Medical Costs and Productivity Losses Due to Interpersonal Violence and Self-Directed Violence." *American Journal of Preventive Medicine , 32*(6): 474–482.

Courtwright, David. 2001. *Forces of Habit: Drugs and the Making of the Modern World*. Cambridge, MA: Harvard University Press.

Cucchiaro, S., J. Ferreira Jr., and A. Sicherman. 1974. *The Effect of the 18-Year-Old Drinking Age on Auto Accidents*. Cambridge, MA: Massachusetts Institute of Technology, Operations Research Center.

D'Emilio, John. 2003. "The Gay Liberation Movement." In Jeff Goodwin and James Jasper (eds.), *The Social Movements Reader*, London: Blackwell, pp. 32–53.

Denzin, Norman. 1987. *The Recovering Alcoholic*. Newbury Park, CA: Sage.

Diekstra, R. F. W. 1982. "Epidemiology of Attempted Suicide in the EEC." In J. Wilmott and J. Mendlewicz (eds.) *New Trends in Suicide Prevention*. New York: Karger, pp. 1–16.

Dill, Bonnie Thornton, and Ruth Zambrana (eds). 2009. *Emerging Intersections: Race, Class, and Gender in Theory, Policy and Practice*. New Jersey: Rutgers University Press.

Donald, M., J. Dower, I. Correa-Velez, and M. Jones. 2006. "Risk and Protective Factors for Medically Serious Suicide Attempts: A Comparison of Hospital-Based With Population-Based Samples of Young Adults." *Aust N Z J Psychiatry, 40*: 87–96.

Douglass, R. L., L. D. Filkins, and F. A. Clark. 1974. *The Effect of Lower Legal Drinking Ages on Youth Crash Involvement*. Ann Arbor: University of Michigan, Highway Safety Research Institute.

Drug Enforcement Administration. 2010. *Fact Sheet: Prescription Drug Abuse*. Retrieved May 10, 2010 (http://www.justice.gov/dea/concern/prescription_drug_fact_sheet.html).

Dube, S. R., F. F. Anda, V. J. Felitti, J. B. Croft, V. J. Edwards, and W. H. Giles. 2001. "Growing Up With Parental Alcohol Abuse: Exposure to Childhood Abuse, Neglect and Household Dysfunction." *Child Abuse and Neglect, 25*: 1627–40.

Durkheim, Emile. 1933. *The Division of Labor in Society*. New York: Macmillan.

———. 1947. *The Elementary Forms of Religious Life*. Glencoe, IL: Free Press.

———. 1951. *Suicide: A Study in Sociology*. New York: Free Press.

Elia, John P. 2003. "Queering Relationships: Toward a Paradigmatic Shift." *Journal of homosexuality, 45*(2–4): 61–86.

Eliason, Michele J. 1996. "Identity Formation for Lesbian, Bisexual, and Gay Persons: Beyond a 'Minoritizing' View." *Journal of Homosexuality, 30*(3): 31–58.

Elliott, Sinikka. 2010. "Parents' Constructions of Teen Sexuality: Sex Panics, Contradictory Discourses, and Social Inequality," *Symbolic Interaction, 33*(2): 191–212.

Enten, Harry. 2007. "More Americans Say They Support Gay Marriage (49%) Than Oppose It (46%)." *Yahoo News*.

Felson, R. B., and K. B. Burchfield. 2004. "Alcohol and the Risk of Physical and Sexual Victimization," *Criminology, 42*(4): 837–59.

Ferrell, Jeff, and Neil Websdale (eds.). 1999. *Making Trouble: Cultural Constructions of Crime, Deviance, and Control*. New York: Aldine de Gruyter.

Finer L. B., and S. K. Henshaw. 2006. "Disparities in Rates of Unintended Pregnancy in the United States, 1994 and 2001." *Perspect Sex Reprod Health, 38*(2): 90–6.

Fisher, B. S., F. T. Cullen, and M. G. Turner. 2000. *The Sexual Victimization of College Women*. Washington, D.C.: The National Institute of Justice and the Bureau of Justice Statistics, U.S. Department of Justice.

Folgero, T. 2008. "Queer Nuclear Families? Reproducing and Transgressing Heteronormativity." *Journal of Homosexuality, 54*(1–2): 124–49.

Fox, J. A., and J. J. Sobol. 2000. "Drinking Patterns, Social Interaction, and Barroom Behavior: A Routine Activities Approach," *Deviant Behavior, 21*(5): 429–50.

Frank, Deborah A., Marilyn Augustyn, Wanda Grant Knight, Tripler Pell, and Barry Zuckerman. 2001. "Growth, Development, and Behavior in Early Childhood Following Prenatal Cocaine Exposure." *Journal of the American Medical Association, 285*: 1613–25.

Gates, Gary J. 2006, "Same-Sex Couples and the Gay, Lesbian, Bisexual Population: New Estimates from the American Community Survey." Retrieved June 1, 2010 (http://gaylife.about.com/od/comingout/a/population.htm).

Gibson, P. 1989. *Gay Male and Lesbian Youth Suicide* (Report of the Secretary's Task Force on Youth Suicide). Washington, D.C.: Alcohol Drug Abuse and Mental Health Administration (ADAMHA), Department of Health and Human Services (DHHS).

Glenn, Norval, and Elizabeth Marquardt. 2001. *Hooking Up, Hanging Out and Hoping for Mr. Right: College Women on Dating and Mating Today.* New York: An Institute for American Values Report to the Independent Women's Forum.

Golub, A., B. D. Johnson, and E. Dunlap. 2005. "Subcultural Evolution and Illicit Drug Use." *Addiction Research and Theory, 13*(3): 217–29.

Golub, Andrew, Bruce D. Johnson, and Erich Labouvie. 2000. "On Correcting Biases in Self-Reports of Age at First Substance Use With Repeated Cross-Section Analysis." *Journal of Quantitative Criminology, 16*(1): 45–68.

Gottfredson, Michael R., and Hirschi, Travis. 1990. *A General Theory of Crime.* Stanford, CA: Stanford University Press.

Graham, Kathryn, and Samantha Wells. 2001. "Aggression Among Young Adults in the Social Context of the Bar," *Addiction Theory and Research, 9*(3): 193–219.

———, and ———. 2003. "'Somebody's Gonna Get Their Head Kicked in Tonight!' Aggression Among Young Males in Bars: A Question of Values." *British Journal of Criminology, 43*: 546–66.

Graham, Kathryn, P. West, and S. Wells. 2000. "Evaluating Theories of Alcohol-Related Aggression Using Observations of Young Adults in Bars," *Addiction, 95*(6): 847–63.

Graham, Kathryn, Wayne D. Osgood, Samantha Wells, and Tim Stockwell. 2006. "To What Extent is Intoxication Associated With Aggression in Bars? A Multilevel Analysis." *Journal of Studies on Alcohol, 67*: 382–90.

Grazian, David. 2009. "Urban Nightlife and the Performance of Masculinity as Collective Activity," *Symbolic Interaction, 30*(2): 221–43.

Guttmacher, Alan. 1994. *Sex and America's Teenagers.* New York: Alan Guttmacher Institute.

Hadfield, Phil. 2006. *Bar Wars: Contesting the Night in Contemporary British Cities.* New York: Oxford University Press.

Harvey, Mike. 2008. "First Cyber-Bullying Trial Hears How Megan Meier, 13, Killed Herself After Online Taunts." November 20. Retrieved June 1, 2010 (www.Times Online. co.uk).

Hirschi, Travis. 1969. *Causes of Delinquency.* Berkeley: University of California Press.

Hobbs, Dick, Philip Hadfield, and Stuart Lister. 2003. *Bouncers: Violence and Governance in the Night-Time Economy*. New York: Oxford University Press.

Holmberg, Mark. 2001. "US VA: Nightclubs in Alphabet Soup with ABC Cracking Down on X." *Richmond Times-Dispatch*, June 6.

Jacobs, Bruce. 1999. *Dealing Crack*. Boston: Northeastern University Press.

Johnson, Bruce, Andrew Golub, and Jeffrey Fagan. 1995. "Careers in Crack: Drug Use, and Drug Distribution in Inner-City Neighborhoods," *Crime and Delinquency, 41*(3): 275–95.

Johnston, L. D., P. M. O'Malley, and J. G. Bachman. 2003. *Monitoring the Future National Survey Results On Drug Use, 1975–2002. Volume II: College Students and Adults Ages 19–40* (NIH Publication No. 03-5376). Bethesda, MD: National Institute on Drug Abuse.

Jones, Marshall B., and Donald R. Jones. 2000. "The Contagious Nature of Antisocial Behavior." *Criminology, 38*: 25–46.

Jureidini, Jon N., Christopher, J. Doecke, Peter R. Mansfield, Michelle M. Haby, David B. Menkes, and Anne L. Tonkin. 2004. "Efficacy and Safety of Antidepressants for Children and Adolescents." *BMJ, 328*: 879–83.

Justice, Emma. 2007, September 15. "Facebook Suicide: The End of a Virtual Life." Posted on September 15, TimesOnline. Retrieved June 1, 2010 (http://women.timesonline.co.uk/tol/life_and_style/women/body_and_soul/article2452928.ece).

Kandel, D. B. 2003. "Does Marijuana Use Cause the Use of Other Drugs?" Editorial. *Journal of the American Medical Association, 289*(4): 482–83.

———, K. Yamaguchi, and L. C. Klein. 2006. "Testing the Gateway hypothesis." (editorial). *Addiction, 101*(4): 470–72.

Kaplan, H. B., S. Martin, and C. Robbins. 1984. "Pathways to Adolescent Drug Use: Self-Derogation, Peer Influence, Weakening of Social Controls, and Early Substance Use," *Journal of Health and Social Behavior, 25*: 270–89.

———, ———, and ———. 1986. "Escalation of Marijuana Use: Application of a General Theory of Deviant Behavior," *Journal of Health and Social Behavior, 27*: 44–61.

Kelleher, K., M. Chaffin, J. Hollenberg, and E. Fischer. 1994. "Alcohol and Drug Disorders Among Physically Abusive and Neglectful Parents in a Community-Based Sample." *American Journal of Public Health, 84*: 1586–90.

Kendall, Diana. 2010. *Social Problems in a Diverse Society*. 5th edition. Boston: Pearson Publishing.

Kimmel, Michael S., and Matthew Mahler. 2007. *Classical Sociological Theory*. New York: Oxford University Press.

Lemert, Edwin M. 2000. *Crime and Deviance: Essays and Innovations of Edwin M. Lemert*. Lanham, MD: Rowan Littlefield.

Leonard, K. E., R. L. Collins, and B. M. Quigley. 2003. "Alcohol Consumption and the Occurrence and Severity of Aggression: An Event-Based Analysis of Male to Male Barroom Violence," *Aggressive Behavior, 29*: 346–65.

Lester, Barry M., Lynne Andreozzi, and Lindsey Appiah. 2004. "Substance Use During Pregnancy: Time For Policy to Catch up With Research." *Harm Reduction Journal, 1*: 1–124.

Lindesmith, Alfred. 1965. *The Addict and the Law*. Bloomington, IN: Indiana University Press.

———. 1968. *Addiction and Opiates*. Chicago: Aldine Publishing Company.

Little, Craig B., and Andrea Rankin. 2001. "Why Do They Start It? Explaining Reported Early-Teen Sexual Activity," *Sociological Forum, 16*(4): 703–29.

Lofland, John. 1969. *Deviance and Identity*. Englewood Cliffs, NJ: Prentice Hall.

Loftus, Jeni. 2001. "America's Liberalization in Attitudes Toward Homosexuality, 1973 to 1998," *American Sociological Review,* October, *66*(5): 762–82.

Lussier, P., J. Proulx, and M. LeBlanc. 2005. "Criminal Propensity, Deviant Sexual Interests, and Criminal Activity of Sexual Aggressors Against Women: A Comparison of Explanatory Models," *Criminology, 43*(1): 249–82.

McCarthy, Bill, and John Hagan. 2001. "When Crime Pays: Capital, Competence and Criminal Success," *Social Forces, 79*(3): 1035–60.

McCraig, L. F., and E. N. Nawar. 2006. *National Hospital Ambulatory Medical Care Survey: 2004 Emergency Department Summary. Advance Data from Vital and Health Statistics No 372*. Hyattsville, MD: National Center for Health Statistics.

MacKay, A. P., L. A. Fingerhut, and C. R. Duran. 2000. *Adolescent Health Chartbook. Health United States*. Hyattsville, MD: National Center for Health Statistics.

MacLeod, Jay. 1987. *Ain't No Makin' It*. Boulder, CO: Westview Press.

Maher, Lisa. 1996. *Sexed Word*. Oxford: University of Oxford Press.

Markowitz, Sara, and Cuellar, Alison. 2007. "Anti-depressants and Youth: Healing or Harmful?" *Social Science & Medicine, 64*(10): 2138–51.

Marsiglia, Flavio F., Stephen Kulis, and Michael Hecht. 2001. "Ethnic Labels And Ethnic Identity as Predictors of Drug Use Among Middle School Students in the Southwest," *Journal of Research on Adolescence, 11*(1): 21–48.

Marx, Karl. 1995 [1867]. *Capital: An Abridged Edition*. New York: Oxford University Press.

———, and Friedrich Engels. 1992 [1848]. *Communist Manifesto*. New York: Oxford University Press.

Maynard, R. A. 1997. *Kids Having Kids: Economic Costs and Social Consequences of Teen Pregnancy*. Washington, DC: The Urban Institute Press. 1997.

Meade, Christina, and Jeannette R. Ickovics. 2005. "Systematic Review of Sexual Risk Among Pregnant and Mothering Teens in the USA: Pregnancy as an Opportunity for Integrated Prevention of STD and Repeat Pregnancy," *Social Science and Medicine, 60*: 661–78.

Measham, Fiona, Judith Aldridge, and Howard Parker. 2001. *Dancing and Drugs: Risk, Health, and Hedonism in the British Club Scene*. London: Free Association.

Merton, Robert K. 1968. *Social Theory and Social Structure*. New York: Free Press.

Miller, Brenda A., Debra Furr-Holden, Robert B. Voas, and Kristin Bright. 2005. "Emerging Adults' Substance Use and Risky Behaviors in Club Settings." *Journal of Drug Issues, 35*: 357–78.

Miller, Jody. 2000. *One of the Guys: Girls, Gangs and Gender*. New York: Oxford University Press.

Moffatt, Michael. 1989. *Coming of Age in New Jersey: College and American Culture*. New Brunswick: Rutgers University Press.

Mohler-Kuo, M., G. Dowdall, and M. P. Koss. 2004. "Correlates of Rape While Intoxicated in a National Sample of College Women," *Journal of Studies on Alcohol, 65*(1): 37–45.

Morrison-Velasco, Sharon. 2000. "Wrapping Around Empathy: The Role of Empathy in the Wraparound Model." *Ethical Human Sciences and Services, 2*: 109–17.

Mosler, Damon. 2001. "Club Drugs." *Law Enforcement Quarterly, 30*(2): 5–10.

NAS (National Academy of Sciences). 2003. *Reducing Underage Drinking: A Collective Responsibility,* Rockville, MD: Institute of Medicine.

NHTSA (National Highway Traffic Safety Administration). 2005. "2005 Drunk Driving Statistics." Retrieved August 23, 2010 (http://www.alcoholalert.com/drunk-driving-statistics-2005.html).

NORML California. 2009. "California Survey Shows Student Marijuana Use Stable, Prescription Drug Use High." Retrieved June 15, 2010 (www.canorml.org/news/css0708.html).

NSDUH (National Survey on Drug Use and Health). 2004. *How Youths Obtain Marijuana.* Rockville, MD: Department of Health and Human Services, Substance Abuse and Mental Health Services Administration, Office of Applied Studies. Retrieved August 23, 2010 (www.samhsa.gov).

———. 2007. *A Day in the Life of American Adolescents: Substance Use Facts.* Rockville, MD: Department of Health and Human Services, Substance Abuse and Mental Health Services Administration, Office of Applied Studies. Retrieved August 23, 2010 (www.samhsa.gov).

———. 2008. *Trends in Substance Use, Dependence or Abuse, and Treatment among Adolescents: 2002 to 2007.* Rockville, MD: Department of Health and Human Services, Substance Abuse and Mental Health Services Administration, Office of Applied Studies. Retrieved August 23, 2010 (www.samhsa.gov).

———. 2009a. *Marijuana and Perceived Risk Among Adolescents: 2002–2007.* Rockville, MD: Department of Health and Human Services, Substance Abuse and Mental Health Services Administration, Office of Applied Studies. Retrieved August 23, 2010 (www.samhsa.gov).

———. 2009b. *Nonmedical Use of Adderall among Fulltime College Students.* Rockville, MD: Department of Health and Human Services, Substance Abuse and Mental Health Services Administration, Office of Applied Studies. Retrieved August 23, 2010 (www.samhsa.gov).

Parks, K. A. 2000. "An Event-Based Analysis of Aggression Women Experience in Bars," *Psychology of Addictive Behaviors, 14*(2): 102–10.

Parsons, Talcott. 1951. *The Social System.* Glencoe, IL: Free Press.

———. 1971. *The System of Modern Societies.* Englewood Cliffs, NJ: Prentice Hall.

Provine, Doris. 2007. *Unequal Under the Law: Race and the War on Drugs.* Chicago: University of Chicago Press.

Quinney, Richard. 1975. *Criminology: Analysis and Critique of Crime in America.* Boston: Little Brown.

Reinarman, Craig, Dan Waldorf, Sheigla Murphy, and Harry Leveine. 1997. "The Contingent Call of the Pipe: Bingeing and Addiction Among Heavy Cocaine Smokers." In Craig Reinarman and Harry Leveine (eds.), *Crack in America.* Berkeley: University of California Press, pp. 77–97.

Remafedi, G., J. Farrow, and R. Deisher. 1991. "Risk Factors for Attempted Suicide in Gay and Bisexual Youth." *Pediatrics, 87*: 869–75.

Richie, Beth E. 2002. "The Social Impact of Mass Incarceration on Women." In M. Mauer and M. Chesney-Lind (eds.), *Invisible Punishment: The Collateral Consequences of Mass Imprisonment.* New York: New Press, pp. 136–49.

Rimmerman, Craig A. 2008. *The Lesbian and Gay Movements.* Boulder, CO: Westview Press.

Robbins, Cynthia. 2007. "Chapter 6. Drug Use and the Family, in Drug Abuse and Society." Unpublished manuscript.

Rosario, M., H. F. L. Meyer-Bahlburg, J. Hunter, T. Exner, M. Gwadz, and A. M. Keller. 1996. "The Psychosexual Development of Urban Lesbian, Gay, and Bisexual Youths." *Journal of Sex Research, 33*(2): 113–26.

Sampson, Robert J., and Stephen W. Raudenbush. 1999. "Systematic Social Observation of Public Spaces: A New Look at Disorder in Urban Neighborhoods," *American Journal of Sociology, 105*(3): 603–51.

Sampson, Robert J., Stephen W. Raudenbush, and Earls Felton. 1997. "Neighborhoods and Violent Crime: A Multilevel Study of Collective Efficacy," *Science, 277*: 918–24.

Shaw, Clifford R., and Henry D. MacKay. 1969. *Juvenile Delinquency and Urban Areas.* Chicago: University of Chicago Press.

Sherley, A. J. 2005. "Contextualizing the Sexual Assault Event: Images From Police Files," *Deviant Behavior, 26*(2): 87–108.

Singer, Lynn, Robert Arendt, Sonia Minnes, Kathleen Farkas, Ann Salvator, Lester Kirchner, and Robert Kliegman. 2002. "Cognitive and Motor Outcomes of Cocaine-Exposed Infants." *The Journal of the American Medical Association, 287*: 1952–60.

Stephens, Richard C. 1991. *Street Addict Roles: A Theory of Heroin Addiction.* Albany, NY: State University of New York Press.

Strouse, Jerimiah S. 1987. "College Bars as Social Settings for Heterosexual Contacts." *Journal of Sex Research, 23*: 374–82.

Terry-McElrath, Yvonne M., Patrick M. O'Malley, and Lloyd D. Johnston. 2009. "Reasons For Drug Use Among American Youth by Consumption Level, Gender, and Race/Ethnicity: 1976–2005." *Journal of Drug Issues, 39*(3): 677–714.

Tjaden, P., and N. Thoennes. 1998. *Prevalence, Incidence, and Consequences of Violence Against Women: Findings from the National Violence Against Women Survey,* Washington, DC: National Institute of Justice, U.S. Department of Justice.

U.S. Senate Subcommittee on Juvenile Justice. 1994. *Shaping Our Responses to Violent and Demeaning Imagery in Popular Music.* Washington, DC: U.S. Government Printing Office.

Valdez, Avelardo. 2002. "Club drugs." *Police: The Law Enforcement Magazine, 26*(4): 74–77.

Venkatesh, Sudhir A. 2000. *American Project: The Rise and Fall of a Modern Ghetto.* Cambridge: Harvard.

Venkatesh, Sudhir A., and Steven D. Levitt. 2000. "'Are we a Family or a Business?' History and Disjuncture in The Urban American Street Gang." *Theory and Society , 29*(4): 427–62.

Ventura, S. J., J. C. Abma, W. D. Mosher, and, S. K. Henshaw. 2006. *Recent Trends in Teenage Pregnancy in the United States, 1990–2002.* National Center for Health Statistics. Health E-Stat. Retrieved August 23, 2010 (www.cdc.gov/nchs/products/pubs/pubd/hestats/teenpreg1990-2002/teenpreg1990-2002.htm.2006).

Wagenaar, A. C. 1983. *Alcohol, Young Drivers, and Traffic Accidents.* Lexington, MA: Lexington Books.

———. 1993. "Minimum Drinking Age and Alcohol Availability to Youth: Issues and Research Needs." in M. E. Hilton and G. Bloss (eds.), *Economics and the Prevention of Alcohol-Related Problems.* National Institute on Alcohol Abuse and Alcoholism (NIAAA) Research Monograph No. 25, NIH Pub. No. 93-3513. Bethesda, MD: NIAAA: 175–200.

Wagenaar, A. C. and M. Wolfson. 1995. "Deterring Sales and Provision of Alcohol to Minors: A Study of Enforcement In 295 Counties in Four States." *Public Health Rep., 110*: 419–27.

Wechsler, H., and E. S. Sands. 1980. "Minimum-Age Laws and Youthful Drinking: An Introduction." In H. Wechsler (ed.), *Minimum Drinking Age Laws*. Lexington, MA: Lexington Books, pp. 1–10.

Weinberg, Martin S., Colin J. Williams, and Douglas W. Pryor, 1994. *Dual Attraction: Understanding Bisexuality*. New York: Oxford University Press.

Whitehead, P. C. 1977. *Alcohol and Young Drivers: Impact and Implications of Lowering the Drinking Age*. Ottawa: Department of National Health and Welfare, Health Protection Branch, Nonmedical use of Drugs Directorate, Research Bureau.

Whitehead, P. C., J. Craig, N. Langford, C. MacArthur, B. Stanton, and R. G. Ferrence. 1975. "Collision Behavior of Young Drivers: Impact of the Change in the Age of Majority." *J Stud Alcohol, 36*: 1208–23.

Williams, A. F., R. F. Rich, P. L. Zador, and L. S. Robertson. 1974. *The Legal Minimum Drinking Age and Fatal Motor Vehicle Crashes*. Washington, DC: Insurance Institute for Highway Safety.

Wright, Eric R., and Brea L. Perry. 2006. "Sexual Identity Distress, Social Support, and the Health of Gay, Lesbian, and Bisexual Youth", *Journal of Homosexuality, 51*(1): 81–110.

Yoder, K. A., Hoyt, D. R., and Whitbeck, L. B. 1998. "Suicidal Behavior Among Homeless and Runaway Adolescents." *Journal of Youth and Adolescence, 27*(6): 753–71.

YRBS (Youth Risk Behavior Surveillance). 2004. *Morbidity and Mortality Weekly Report 53*/No. SS-2. Retrieved February 1, 2007 (http://www.cdc.gov/mmwr).

Ziemba, Autumn. 2010. "D.A.R.E. Police Officer Busts Kid After Accidental Text," May 16. Retrieved May 16, 2010 (www.foxnews.com).

Glossary/Index

60 Minutes 31

A
abovetheinfluence.com 51–52
Add Health
    see National Longitudinal Study of Adolescent Health Survey (also referred to as
       Add Health)
Adderall 31
Agnew, Robert 5
alcohol
    advertising aimed at youth 2
    conflicting messages on 2
    costs of underage drinking 20–21, 21t
    demographic patterns in use of 25–26
    extent of abuse among youth and young adults 22
    facilitating hook ups 17–18
    GLBT teens use of 16–17
    hospital visits as a result of 21
    involvement in traffic-related injuries 20
    legal drinking age 2
    in nightclubs and bars 32–33
    pregnant women's use of 27
    use in search for identity 29, 51
alienation: a state of detachment from society's norms and a theory of deviant moti-
    vation that people are naturally law-abiding; people break rules because of strain,
    and strain originates in our social experience 5, 29, 51
altruistic suicide: a type of suicide that results from excessive community control or
    regulation over individuals and their freedoms 38
anomie: coined by Emile Durkheim, anomie refers to the absence of social ties that
    bind people to society, a state where norms about good and bad have little salience

in people's lives. This is also known as 'strain' and it is the basis for strain theory. 4, 5

anti-depressants 36

assimilation: commonly referred to as the forfeiting of a group's unique cultural elements when it gains acceptance into the mainstream. Adopting the cultural customs of the dominant or conventional group in a society. 16

B

binge drinking: refers to an excessive amount of alcohol consumed in an episode of drinking, indicating that one had surpassed norms about how much to drink on any occasion. In the U.S., binge drinking is defined for men as five or more drinks on one occasion and four or more for women. 26, 32

bisexual: a term used to describe sexual attraction to and sexual behavior with both men and women 15

Bourdieu, Pierre 8, 29

Brea, Perry L. 16, 17

Bronfenbrenner, Urie 14

C

capital 8, 29–30

capitalism 4, 7

causality 41–42

child sexual abuse 12–13, 28, 40

Clueless 11

cocaine 31, 33

collectivism: a set of beliefs common to a group of people that give them a strong sense of belonging to a community or society 38

concepts: words or symbols used to represent our mental images-or conceptions- of a collection of related phenomena. Sociologists turn them into observable variables. 3

conflict theory: a major sociological theory that views society as an arena of inequality and conflict. Conflict theories are macro-oriented like structural functionalists, but they are nearly opposite on how that structure originates and functions. For conflict theorists, society's structure is controlled by those with the greatest economic, social, and cultural assets. 4, 7–8, 49–50

crack cocaine 27

crime

and drug use 33–34

nightclubs as sites of 32

non-medical prescription drugs and implications in 31

substance abuse parents in criminal justice system 28

and underage drinking 21t

youth delinquency 4–5

cultural diversity: variation among people due to the cultural heritages and customs that accompany their race, ethnicity, class, gender, and sexual orientation 7, 10

cyber-bullying: refers to the use of the Internet, cell phones or other devices to send or post hurtful text or images that would embarrass another person 35, 42

D

dependent variable: a factor that one seeks to explain or predict, one whose outcome is influenced by other variables 9, 41, 42

deviant careers: a set of deviant or non-normative behaviors, roles, and identities that comprise a lifestyle, running counter to conventional society in some ways and consistent in others **6**, 23

deviant identities: definitions of the self centered on violating social norms or embracing non-conventional ways 6

drinking age, legal 2

drugs 26–27

    cocaine 31, 33

    crack cocaine 27

    and crime 33–34

    dealing 5, 24–25, 29, 30, 33

    demographic patterns in use of 10, 24–25, 26–27, 51

    ecstasy 33

    extent of abuse among youth and young adults 22–23

    linking psychotherapeutic drugs and suicide 36

    in nightclubs and bars 33

    pregnant women and abuse of 27

    prescription drug abuse 30–31, 34, 44

    prevention programs 51

    use in search for identity 28–30, 41, 51

    see also marijuana

Durkheim, Emile 4, 5, 38, 49

E

Ecological Systems Theory 14

ecstacy 33

egoistic suicide: a type of suicide that occurs when people are not effectively tied to others in society or the ways of it; too much detachment of the individual 38–39

Elliott, Sinikka 11

environmental model: focuses on reducing the availability of opportunities for problem behavior. These programs focus on community characteristics and the interplay of laws, policies, commercial establishments, and social institutions therein. 48–50, 51

environmental or macro factors: a broad focus on structures that shape society as whole 3, 4, 7, 9

ethnographic study: a qualitative research effort that investigates the phenomena or subjects where they are naturally found. It collects a wide variety of mostly textual or narrative data on people's lives as they actually live them. 32

F

Facebook 39

families

and preventative programs for youth problems 50

risks to children of substance abuse within 27–28, 40

family transmission thesis: the idea that a parent's behaviors are transmitted to their children. It is commonly used to describe deviant behaviors. For example, children who were abused by their parents become abusers of children themselves later in life. 28

Feinstein, Diana 25

femininity (traditional): identity expectations, usually for biological females to adopt the traits of compassion, empathy, dependence, and cooperation with others 41

financial capital 8, 29

Focalin 31

funding and resources for youth programs 45–46

G

gateway hypothesis: the notion that use of some illicit drugs, e.g., marijuana, leads to abuse of harder ones, e.g., cocaine and heroin. It describes the phenomenon in which an introduction to drug-using behavior through the use of tobacco, alcohol, or marijuana is related to subsequent use of other illicit drugs. The theory suggests that, all other things being equal, an adolescent who uses any one drug is more likely to use another drug. Under this hypothesis, tobacco, alcohol, and marijuana are all considered "gateway drugs," preceding the use of one another and of illicit drugs. 23

gay: a term used to describe same-sex attraction and sexual behavior, i.e., homosexual. It is often used to refer to male homosexuals in particular. 15–17

gender

connection with identity development and sexuality 36, 41

difference in suicide patterns 37

differences in drug use motivations 26–27

sexual assault patterns by 18

GLBT youth 15–17
Gottfredson, Michael R. 6

H
heavy drinking: in the U.S., this term refers to binge-level drinking on five or more days a week 26, 32
heteronormative: when the beliefs, values, and social arrangements and practices conform to heterosexuality, using them as a standard to judge all sexualities and interactions 41
Hirschi, Travis 6, 7
HIV: human immunodeficiency virus (HIV) is a blood-borne retrovirus contracted through bodily fluids via unprotected sex, needle-sharing, or blood transfusions. It is the cause of AIDS, which is a fatal disease. 14, 19, 44, 47
homophobia: intolerance or an intense fear and hatred of homosexuals. Also includes bias and discrimination against homosexuals. 16
homosexuality 15–17
hooking up: a new form of intimate interaction that features a wide range of consensual sexual behavior with no expectation for a relationship. Common to college students and youth. 17–18, 19
hot spots: a term used by criminologists to describe geographic areas high in crime 32
human capital 8, 30
hypotheses: a set of statements, with independent and dependent variables, about what one expects to find in the research process 41

I
identity
    adolescent development of 19, 36, 40–41
    defining one's sexual 11, 15–16, 19
    development and connection with sexuality and gender 36, 41
    ethnic 51
    and multi-identities 10
    substance abuse in search for 28–30, 41, 51
independent variable: a force or factor whose manipulation produces a change in a subsequent force or factor 9, 41, 42
individual or micro-level explanation: these explain youth problems by using characteristics or experiences of individuals. They are also known as social-psychological theories. Since these theories focus on individuals, they can be developed using traditional scientific methods (quantitative and qualitative studies). These theories also often help identity the causes, or in other words, the independent variable. 3, 4, 5, 9

information model: educating people about the dangers and consequences associated with certain behaviors so that they do not engage in them 48

intersectionality: the idea that people have different life experiences due to their unique combinations of race, class, and gender traits 10, 51–52

IS PATH WARM 38, 40

J
Juvenile Delinquency and Control Act 1961 49

K
Kemp, Jack 49

L
labeling theory: a social process theory that says the way that society labels certain acts as deviant is seen as the primary condition of deviance. It is a direct descendant of symbolic interactionism. 6, 24

and preventative programs 46, 50, 51

lesbian: a term used to describe same-sex attraction to and sexual behavior between women 15

life skills model: attempts to get people to turn their newfound knowledge on the dangers of certain behaviors into concrete, positive action 48, 50–51

M
marijuana 22–23, 31

and debate over progression to hard drugs after use of 23–24, 33–34

demographic patterns in use of 24–25

lobby to decriminalize 7

use in nightclubs and bars 33

youth methods of obtaining 25

masculinity (traditional): identity expectations, usually for biological males to adopt the traits of assertiveness, strength, independence, and risk-taking 41

Mean Girls 11

medicalization: the process through which non-medical behaviors and traits are redefined or classified and treated as medical conditions 54

Megan's Law: known at the Federal level as the Sexual Offender Act of 1994. Refers to U.S. laws that require law enforcement officials to make information available to the public regarding registered sex offenders. The states vary in what information will be made available (e.g., offender's name, picture, address, incarceration date, and nature of crime) and how it will be disseminated (e.g., websites, newspapers). 12

Meier, Megan 35–36, 42

Merton, Robert 4–5, 8, 29, 49

micro-level: factors or explanations that focus on individual or small group traits, behaviors, and experiences 3

Monitoring the Future Study: an annual survey of high school drug use sponsored by the National Institute on Drug Abuse and conducted at the University of Michigan. Its purpose is to gauge annual prevalence and frequency of drug use among the nation's youth. It began in the mid-1970s. 22, 26

moral crusade: a social movement campaign around a symbolic issue based in morality (e.g., prohibition) 2

moral entrepreneurs: powerful or influential people who campaign for moral issues they endorse in an attempt to make them binding on a wider population 17

moral panic: refers to the reaction of a group of people (but not a social movement) based on the false belief that another sub-culture or a group poses danger to the society. The major impetus for these panics is provided by the media. Moral panic is often expressed as anger rather than fear. 20

N

National Crime Victimization Survey (NCVS): a national survey of U.S. households on crime victimization and its characteristics. Conducted annually by the Bureau of Justice. 18

National Longitudinal Study of Adolescent Health Survey (also referred to as AddHealth): a longitudinal study of a nationally representative sample of adolescents in grades 7-12 in the United States during the 1994-95 school year. It offers useful information on how environmental factors influence youth behaviors, especially those related to health. 22

National Survey on Drug Use and Health: administered by the Substance Abuse and Mental Health Services Association (SAMHSA), this is the primary source of information on the prevalence, patterns, and consequences of drug and alcohol use and abuse. It is administered to U.S. households annually and tracks substance use, dependency and related behaviors among people aged 12–94. 22

nightclubs and bars 18, 32–33

Nixon, Richard 49

non-medical use of prescription drugs: according to the NSDUH (2009: 3), "Non-medical use is defined as the use of prescription-type drugs not prescribed for the respondent by a physician or used only for the experience or feeling they cause." 30–31, 34, 44

P

parents, substance-abusing 27–28, 40

Parsons, Talcott 4

patterning 9–10, 11
    of sexual assault 18
    for substance abuse 10, 24–27, 51
    for suicide 37–38

personal capital: a desire for wealth, risk-taking propensity, willingness to cooperate, and competence 30

physical assault 33, 41

pregnancy
    and substance abuse 27
    teen 13–14

prescription painrelievers: narcotics prescribed by a medical doctor to reduce pain and suffering. Most are opiates. 30–31, 34, 44

prevention programs: programs that try to stop problem behavior before it ever occurs or to slow it down before it becomes too problematic 45
    as a key to combating youth social problems 46–48
    sociologists' role in 48–52

primary prevention: attempts to stop problems before they happen in the first place. Mostly used with youth. 47

prison 28

private agencies 45–46

proscriptive prevention programs: similar to punishment in that they increase the costs and penalties associated with problematic behavior. 48

punishment policies: punitive policies that formally hold people accountable to sanctions 45

Q

qualitative methods: designed to capture greater detail about the research topic. These approaches can include interviews, focus groups, or participant observation. 8–9

quantitative methods: designed to capture more specific information that is most often expressed in numbers, statistics, or distinct categories. These approaches can include surveys or experiments. 8–9

queer theory: a critical theory developed from the ideas of Michel Foucault that claims gender and sexuality are fluid and socially constructed. The theory holds that no sexualities are wrong, but that those other than heterosexuality are deemed deviant in society for largely political purposes. 16

R

race
    drug use and 10, 24, 27, 51
    and identity problems 51

suicide patterns and 37–38

rape 18, 33, 41, 46

Reefer Madness 25

rehabilitation and re-entry programs: programs that attempt to change law-breakers, who have previously been punished by society, into conforming citizens free of problem behavior 45

Reno, Janet 49

research methods, sociological 8–9

risk factors: phenomena (e.g., traits, events, and experiences) believed to elevate the likelihood that something else, e.g., suicide, will happen 14, 38

Ritaline 31

rite of passage: a cultural concept referring to a ritual event or ceremony that marks a shift in status, including age or stage of human development 23

S

secondary prevention: prevention programs targeted at youth considered at high risk for problem behavior 47

self-fulfilling prophecy: prediction that directly or indirectly causes itself to become true. In this context, the internalization of negative labels leads to adopting deviant roles (i.e., tasks, behaviors) and identities (definitions of the self). 6

self-help groups 46, 47

self-inflicted injuries 37

sexual assault: often referred to as rape, i.e., unlawful carnal knowledge of one person by another, and is legally defined differently by state. Can have multiple degrees. 18, 33, 41, 46

sexual identity 11, 19
    and coming out 15–16

sexual victimization: a term representing a wide range of inappropriate, unwanted and illegal acts of a sexual nature, including rape, child sexual abuse/incest, sexual harassment, stalking, marital rape and domestic violence 12–13, 28, 40

sexuality 11–19
    connection with identity development and gender 36
    connections to substance abuse and suicide 32–33, 39–42
    exploration in high school of 13–14, 15
    of GLBT youth 15–17
    hooking up 17–18, 19
    self-help groups for 46
    and sexual assault 18, 33, 41, 46
    and sexual victimization 12–13, 28, 40

sexually transmitted diseases (STDs): diseases that are spread via sexual acts, including chlamydia, herpes, syphilis, gonorrhea, human papilloma viruses (HPV), etc. 14

social capital 8, 30

social conflict paradigm: see **conflict theory**

    solutions to youth problems 49–50

social constructionism 5, 9, 44

social control theory: a social process theory that proposes that exploiting the process of socialization and social learning builds self-control and reduces the inclination to indulge in behavior recognized as antisocial. It explains primary deviance. 6–7, 50

social learning theory 28, 50–51

social norms model: changing problematic beliefs and values that may have been passed on through generations so conforming behavior results 48, 50

social problems work: the actions done by people and groups to address the behavior and consequences they believe are problematic in society 44

social problems workers: people who have paying jobs and careers working in many capacities to combat social problems, e.g., drug counselors, child protective service caseworkers, agency directors and administrators, etc. 44

social process theories: a category of sociological theories that focuses on how people or groups become involved with deviance, how their involvement changes over time, and what might initiate that change. They concern deviant behavior and identification. 5–6

social reproduction theory 7–8, 29–30

sociology

    sociological research methods 8–9

    and view of youth social problems 2–8

sociology solutions to youth problems 44–52

    based on differing theories 48–52

    prevention as key to 46–48

    types of 45–46

solidarity: describes the state of integration of or sense of belonging among people and groups in society 4, 49

stigma: a mark of disgrace or infamy; a stain or reproach, as on one's reputation 6, 16

strain theory 5, 8, 29

structural functionalism: one of three sociological paradigms relating to substance abuse theories that adopts a macro view of society as a complex system whose parts work together to promote solidarity and stability. It seeks out the "structural" aspects of the social system under consideration, and then studies the processes that function to maintain social structures. In this context, structure primarily refers to normative patterns of behavior (regularized patterns of action in accordance with norms), whilst function explains how such patterns operate as systems. 4–5

dating and traditional courtship consistent with 17

and environmental prevention programs 48–49

on homosexuality 15, 16

substance abuse 20–34

among GLBT teens 16–17

connections to sexuality and suicide 32–33, 39–42

explaining youth 26–27

extent of youth 22–23

family 27–28, 40

in nightclubs and bars 32–33

patterns of 10, 24–27, 51

prescription drug abuse 30–31, 34, 44

programs 47, 50

in search for identity 28–30, 41, 51

social problem or rite of passage debate on 23–24, 33–34

suicide 35–43

connections to sexuality and substance abuse 32–33, 39–42

explanations of 38–39

extent in modern society 36–37

homophobia and links to GLTB teens' attempts at 16

lifetime costs of 37

Megan Meier case 35–36, 42

patterns 37–38

and relationship with psycho-therapeutic drugs 36

self-help groups for people considering 46

structural functionalist analysis of 4–5

suicide ideation: thinking, imaging, or contemplating self-injury or suicide 35, 37

Superbad 11, 13

symbolic interaction: one of three major sociological paradigms relating to substance abuse theories that takes a more micro-level orientation to deviance and drugs, or a more close-up focus on social interaction in specific situations. It sees society as a product of the everyday interactions of individuals, and people act toward things based on the meaning those things have for them. The majority of interactionist research uses qualitative research methods, like participant observation, to study aspects of social interaction and/or individuals' selves. 4, 5–7, 46, 50–51

and explaining sexual assault 18

on homosexuality 15–16

view on youth substance abuse 24

T

teen pregnancy 13–14

teratogenic effects: birth defects that stymie human development, especially of new-borns and young children 27

Terry-McElrath, Karen 26, 27

tertiary prevention: attempts to get people who have histories of problem behavior to cease their activities in both the short and long term 47

theory: an interrelated set of statements that describe how some aspect of social life works. From theory, researchers develop hypotheses, which are statements about the relationships between two or more theoretical constructs or variables. 3

treatment programs: programs that try to fix the physical and mental symptoms, conditions and consequences of problem behavior 45

U

Uniform Drinking Age Act 1984 2

urban legends: hoaxes, rumors, or myths passed on through time that have little basis in fact, yet are highly influential of popular beliefs 25

V

virtual suicide: refers to removing one's internet presence, taking down one's profile from Facebook or MySpace 39

W

website (abovetheinfluence.com) 51–52

wraparound models: a long-term and broad approach that features the coordination of a range of services for those impacted by social problems. Numerous services are provided simultaneously and in all aspects of life, such as family therapy, vocational training, parenting classes, substance abuse counseling, etc. 50

Wright, Eric R. 16, 17

Y

youth programs
    based on differing theories 48–52
    people and resources behind 45–46
    prevention as key to 46–48

Youth Risk Behavior Survey: a school survey conducted annually by the Centers for Disease Control, the Youth Risk Behavior Surveillance System (YRBSS) monitors the health risk behaviors of youth and young adults 22

An environmentally friendly book printed and bound in England by www.printondemand-worldwide.com

PEFC Certified

This product is
from sustainably
managed forests
and controlled
sources

www.pefc.org

This book is made entirely of sustainable materials; FSC paper for the cover and PEFC paper for the text pages.

#0613 - 260613 - C0 - 254/178/4 - PB